Light for Art's Sake

This book is dedicated to my wonderful family: Liz, Ken, Maureen, Rob, Maria, Kurtis, Hannah, and Jessica.

Light for Art's Sake

Lighting for Artworks and Museum Displays

Christopher Cuttle

AMSTERDAM • BOSTON • HEIDELBERG • LONDON • NEW YORK • OXFORD • PARIS
SAN DIEGO • SAN FRANCISCO • SINGAPORE • SYDNEY • TOKYO

Butterworth-Heinemann is an imprint of Elsevier

Butterworth-Heinemann is an imprint of Elsevier
Linacre House, Jordan Hill, Oxford OX2 8DP, UK
30 Corporate Drive, Suite 400, Burlington, MA 01803, USA

First edition 2007

British Library Cataloguing in Publication Data
A catalogue record for this book is available from the British Library

Library of Congress Cataloguing in Publication Data
A catalogue record for this book is available from the Library of Congress

ISBN–13: 978-0-7506-6430-1
ISBN–10: 0-7506-6430-4

For information on all Butterworth-Heinemann publications
visit our web site at http://books.elsevier.com

Typeset by Charon Tec Ltd (A Macmillan Company), Chennai, India
www.charontec.com

Printed and bound in Italy

07 08 09 10 11   10 9 8 7 6 5 4 3 2 1

'Art for art's sake, with no purpose, for any purpose perverts art. But art achieves a purpose which is not its own.'

Benjamin Constant, 1767–1834,
diary, 11 February 1804

'The painting must reveal itself in different aspects if the moods of light are included in its viewing, in its seeing.'

Louis Isadore Kahn, 1901–1974,
Light is the Theme.

Contents

Preface

People visit museums to experience objects rather than images, and among museums, the art museum provides for a special type of visual experience. Visitors want not only to see the object, but to gain an understanding of its nature and the artist's intention in creating it. The underlying concept of this book is that lighting does not merely make things visible, but that it influences the appearance of everything we see. The nature of the lighting is inseparable from the visual experience of art.

I have spent an entire working life in lighting, held by fascination for the manifold ways in which light's interactions with matter inform and guide our lives. I have had opportunities to visit art museums in Europe, North America, Asia, and Australasia, and these experiences have provided a rich foundation for my teaching as well as the basis for this text. This book contains more than 200 of my own photographs gathered in these travels, and I should add a few words of explanation. Readers who are accustomed to seeing the work of professional architectural photographers may be surprised by the casual, almost snapshot, appearance of some of these photographs. The point is that many of them have been taken when I was simply a ticket-holding visitor to the museum, and what I am showing is what a visitor sees. These photographs do not aim to show the art or the architecture, but rather selected aspects of the many different ways in which lighting influences the visual experience of art. Some truly interesting examples that I have seen are omitted because the institution concerned chooses not to allow visitors to take photographs. Occasionally I have requested photographs from such institutions, but they are seldom satisfactory. The precise alignment of the architectural geometry that they portray, and the total lack of human beings or even signs of their contact, creates, to my mind, an artificial appearance. However, the really damning factor is that almost invariably these photographers seem to be unable to resist the temptation of adding photoflood lighting, and of course, that completely defeats my purpose. So I ask readers to be tolerant of my hand-held photographs, and to appreciate that what I am showing is what visitors see.

This book is intended for architects, exhibition designers, lighting professionals, conservation scientists, and museum staff whose work involves them in museum display generally, and in the presentation of art in particular. Generally, the aim of the book is to bring the level of understanding of the visual effects of lighting in museums closer to the current level of understanding of its damaging effects.

Christopher Cuttle

Acknowledgments

I have researched this topic for more than twenty years, during which time I have travelled extensively and discussed museum lighting with many knowledgeable enthusiasts. While I can never make this list complete, I know that it would be incomplete without mention of Gordon Anson, Larry Bowers, Peter Boyce, Howard Brandston, Hervé Cabezas, Stephen Cannon-Brookes, Jim Druzik, Jean-Jacques Ezrati, Frank Florentine, Phil Gabriel, Barry Gasson, Marvin Gelman, Ken Gorbey, Heinrich Kramer, Joe Lynes, Mark Major, Stefan Michalski, Naomi Miller, Mecky Ne'eman, Derek Phillips, Toby Raphael, Mark Rea, Margaret Reid, Joachim Ritter, Edwin Robinson, Paul Ruffles, David Saunders, Rainer Schrammer, Kevan Shaw, André Tammes and Steve Weintraub.

I also acknowledge Paul Gilbert for welcoming me into his photography studio, and Vicki-Anne Heikell and Julia Gresson helping me to obtain photographic material.

Introduction

The presentation of art has become a high-profile industry. Themed exhibitions comprising artworks gathered from many lending organizations are presented by major art institutions and arouse levels of public interest comparable with mass entertainment. Professional exhibition designers are engaged for staging these events, and the quality of the visual presentation that they achieve has come to set the standard for museums around the world.

While many types of institutions need to achieve effective visual communication, museums have a problem that is unique. The light that stimulates vision also causes permanent damage to many museum exhibits, and this includes most forms of art media. Preventive conservation is the discipline concerned with the processes that affect museum objects over time, and the museum professionals of that discipline have made important contributions to preserving our artistic heritage for future generations. This book aims to provide a basis for a similar level of professional expertise for lighting practice in museums. Rather than portraying conservation and display as having diametrically opposed objectives, the aim of this book is to lead all of the professionals concerned to consider how the overall viewing situation may be optimized for the nature of display that is envisaged, and for the lighting designer to devise a means for achieving this with minimal light exposure of the displayed objects.

The purpose for putting museum objects on display is to provide for a pleasurable and informative visual experience, and this involves far more than simply applying a recommended lux level. It requires the lighting designer to identify what are the visible attributes of the displayed objects, and to devise a distribution of lighting that will effectively reveal them. An optimum situation for a light-responsive object is one for which the lighting is specifically suited to the physical characteristics of the object, and provides for a visual experience that satisfies viewers with minimum light exposure of the object. For highly light-responsive objects, degradation should be controlled by limiting the duration of exposure rather than by compromising the quality of presentation.

A philosophy for the presentation of art

1

How should art be presented to enable it to be appreciated by viewers? There is no uniquely correct answer, and clearly this question involves more than just lighting. However, it is a tenet of this book that lighting does not merely make things visible, but that it affects their appearance, and for artworks, this implies that it will affect viewers' appreciation of the artworks.

All museums aim to provide visitors with a visual experience that meets their expectations, and the emphasis in this book upon viewing art is because, in the author's experience, it is in art museums that viewers' expectations are most critical. However, it would be true to say that virtually all of the aspects of lighting that are discussed have relevance to museum lighting in general.

It follows that anyone who becomes involved in providing lighting for museum displays, and particularly lighting for art, needs to give thought to how the nature of the lighting that they will provide may influence the viewers' experience.

We consider below several possible, and even plausible, options.

To make the artwork appear as it would have appeared to the artist at the time of its creation

Rembrandt had his studio on the top floor of his home in Amsterdam, where he lived between 1639 and 1658. The house is now a popular tourist destination and the studio is shown in Figure 1.1. The large windows to the left are north facing, so that the studio receives only diffused sunlight from the sky. The scene shown replicates Rembrandt's preferred arrangement for painting, as inferred from his portraits, including a self-portrait at work. His subject would be seated close to a window in the shallow alcove formed by the fireplace, and he would take up the posture natural for a right-handed artist. He would look at the subject over the palette held in his left hand, with the easel to his right, turned to also catch the light from the windows. A survey of a volume of Rembrandt's *oeuvre* confirms that again and again his subjects are depicted with a strong flow of light from the left, the direction of flow being approximately 45 degrees above the

Facing page: *National Gallery of Art, West Building, Washington DC*

Figure 1.1: *Rembrandt's studio on the top floor of his Amsterdam home (with permission, Rembrandt Museum)*

horizontal. Some impression of the modelling created by this lighting can be gained from the appearance of the bust on the upper shelf. The white sheet over the subject's chair could have been employed as a blind to restrict the light, or as a diffusing reflector. Presumably he used it to regulate the light level throughout the day, and while we can only guess at how he would have done this, it is clear that for his work he wanted an abundance of daylight that was both directional, in the sense of having a distinct flow, and diffused, in the sense of not causing sharply defined shadows.

Figure 1.2: *Paul Cezanne's* atelier *on the outskirts of Aix-en-Provence (with permission, Atelier Cezanne)*

By the time Paul Cezanne built his house in 1902 on a rise on the outskirts of Aix-en-Provence, France, glassmaking technology had advanced to make available large panes of clear glazing. Like Rembrandt, Cezanne devoted the upper floor of his home to his *atelier*, but he was able to use large panes to create an extensive north-facing wall of glass, part of which is shown in Figure 1.2. On the opposite south-facing wall there are domestic-scale windows fitted with shutters to enable him to control the balance of light within the studio, but however these might have been adjusted, the lighting in this space would have been dominated by the powerful flow of diffused light from the north-facing glazing. Even on a dull day, light levels would be high in this space, and perhaps that was Cezanne's intention for he preferred work in the outdoors, and considered studio work to be a substitute for use during poor weather.

It is when we turn attention to the *plein air* artists that we really encounter artworks being created in an abundance of light. Claude Monet painted many scenes on the River Seine, and he set up his studio boat for this work. His friend Edouard Manet captured him at work in his own characteristic style (Figure 1.3), where it can be seen that Monet has made some effort to protect

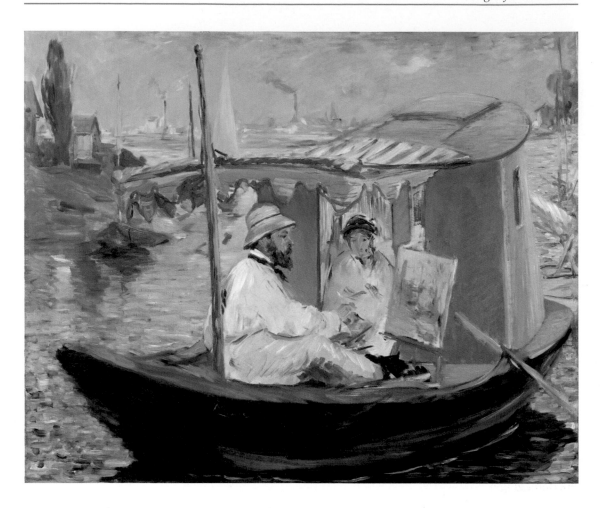

Figure 1.3: *Edouard Manet,*
Monet painting on his
studio boat, *1874 (With
permission, Bayerische
Staatsgemäldesmmlungen,
Neue Pinakothek, München)*

himself from exposure to summer sunlight by erecting a striped
awning and donning a straw hat. It may also be noted that he
has not rolled up his sleeves or removed his tie! However, while
he appears quite relaxed and absorbed in his work, his wife,
Camille, has decided that the level of exposure that he is subject-
ing himself to is far too much for her complexion. The shadow
pattern is not clear so perhaps the sun was obscured by a cloud,
but it may be noted that Monet usually painted facing towards
the light, which would tend to have the effect of shading his canvas. Even so, the light level on the canvas probably would have
been in the order of 50 000 lux; the colour temperature would
have been in the range 6000 to 12 000 K; and the ultraviolet
exposure level would have been very high.

It is widely recognized that museums have to both avoid ultraviolet
exposure and restrict light exposure in order to protect the objects
they display from fading and other forms of degradation. The
processes that may be initiated or accelerated by light exposure

are reviewed in Chapter 3, but is sufficient at this stage to state that museums cannot display objects in lighting conditions that come even close to the conditions in which these artists created their works. The artists themselves chose lighting conditions which would have had the effect of making their works appear altogether brighter and more colourful than the conditions that responsible museums employ. This difference is well understood by museum staff, and their own experts who work on restoration subject the objects to several thousand lux to ensure they have optimum visibility for their delicate work, and this is deemed to be acceptable because these conditions are maintained for only a few weeks at the most. Unfortunately for the rest of us, such conditions are not acceptable for long-term display.

To ensure that no damage due to light exposure will occur

As well as displaying their collections, museums have the responsibility to conserve them, which means that any change in the physical condition or chemical composition of an object represents damage, and must be avoided. There are many ways in which damage may occur, so that protection from the effects of light exposure is only one aspect of overall conservation policies. However, it is a difficult aspect to reconcile because there is no 'safe' level of exposure. It is a cold, hard fact that if an object is even slightly responsive to exposure to light, then exposure at even a very low light level will, in time, cause damage. Museum staff have to face the unpalatable fact that if you can see it, they are damaging it.

The principal underlying theme of this book concerns how to satisfy viewers' expectations for visually experiencing museum objects, and particularly artworks, while causing minimal damage to the objects. The keys to resolving this are understanding how much light is needed for the human visual system to operate satisfactorily, and how this light may be distributed for optimum visual effect. The outcome of applying these principles is that one generation may pass on to the succeeding generation the treasures for which it has had guardianship without having caused unreasonable damage.

To achieve the best possible appearance of the artwork

Most of the lighting techniques that are used in museums, as well as much of the lighting equipment, derive from practices developed for merchandise displays. For these applications, the aims are to catch the viewer's attention and to make the displayed objects appear attractive and appealing. Undoubtedly there are displays in museums for which these are reasonable aims, but to employ such an approach on a widespread basis raises ethical questions. We live in an age when people are routinely exposed to media that are explicitly designed to cut through a cacophony of images, and by comparison a display that shows objects without emphasis or drama may appear dull. It is tempting to use the tools of the marketeers to draw the populace into museums.

The people who use merchandise display techniques effectively are able to make colours appear brighter, shiny surfaces appear more glossy, and transparent materials appear to sparkle. These skills are the stock-in-trade of high street window dressers, and such trickery deserves to be shunned by museum lighting designers. Nonetheless, it needs to be recognized that lighting substantially influences how well the visible attributes of displayed objects are revealed. We will examine this carefully in the following chapter, for another theme of this book is that a skilled lighting designer will appraise what are the critical visible attributes of the objects to be displayed, and will devise lighting that has the qualities to reveal these attributes. There are some fine judgements to be made. How far can one take revealing before it becomes exaggeration? And if we selectively reveal certain attributes, are we at the same time obscuring other features that we have judged to be less worthy? Are we manipulating the situation to present the viewer with an image rather than a view? Lighting is a powerful tool, and ethics is a real issue for museum lighting designers.

To provide optimum conditions for viewing art

A listing of optimum conditions can be drawn up from current knowledge of human vision. Excellent colour rendering is required. The object of regard should be the brightest part of the field of view, with gently graded brightness to the surrounding visual field. There must be a total absence of glare, both direct and reflected. Viewers coming from brighter environments, such as daylight conditions, need to undergo a gradual process of progressive adaptation before entering the viewing space, particularly if low light levels are necessary for conservation reasons. To set up and consistently maintain such conditions generally requires total reliance on electric lighting.

For the viewer who has made a pilgrimage from the other side of the world to visit a collection, or for visitors to a temporary exhibition, it is important to them that nothing should mar the experience of their 'once in a lifetime opportunity'. There is, however, another type of viewing experience that deserves consideration. For the art lover who returns again and again, and for whom the artworks are familiar and much loved objects, to experience the appearance of these objects reflecting the changing moods of season, time of day, and weather, is an integral component of the art lover's interaction with the works. For these viewers, there is no such thing as an optimum visual condition, and the vagaries of daylight are the essence of its appeal.

To impart a sense of having seen 'the real thing'

Anyone who wishes to see the collection of a major museum can find illustrated volumes in their library to peruse, or they can go online and undergo a virtual tour on the museum's website. And yet, people travel vast distances to stand in line and shuffle their way through these institutions' galleries. There is a definite sense of satisfaction to be gained from having seen 'the real thing'. An object as instantly recognizable as the *Mona Lisa* draws endless crowds for whom no quality of reproduction will suffice. To have seen it 'with my own eyes' is the ultimate reality.

As has been discussed, display lighting gives opportunities to manipulate the visual experience, and as people become more exposed to the tricks of merchandise lighting, so they tend to become more mistrustful of what they are being shown. Objects that can be seen only from one direction, and which are isolated from context, and where the source of light is concealed from view, may fail to satisfy. If viewers feel that they want to carry an artwork across to a window to see what it really looks like, the presentation must be regarded as a failure.

Conversely, objects that form part of an overall setting, and where both the objects and the space in which the viewers are located are similarly illuminated, may impart a greater sense of satisfaction. A particular object may be experienced with a sense of intimacy, with every aspect of its physical state visible and recognized. Not only are the desirable attributes revealed, but also any damage or effects of ageing are also clearly visible. This approach may appeal strongly to one's sense of ethics, but there could be a problem: some might judge the appearance dull.

To assist viewers to understand the displayed objects and their reason for being there

Exhibitions, both temporary and permanent, often serve an educational or informative purpose. In fact, it is not uncommon to find that the bottlenecks in a well patronized exhibition form around the text boards rather than the displayed objects. The captions adjacent to the objects can become as important as the objects themselves, and in situations where the illumination levels on the objects are restricted for conservation reasons, it can be difficult to provide for easy reading of the captions without creating brightness contrasts that detract from the displays.

Lighting an object to enable its intrinsic qualities to be understood may lead to a quite different set of specialized lighting objectives. Within an exhibition of an artist's work, there may be some objects on display for which the aim is to reveal the artist's technique, calling for lighting that clearly shows detail of the brushwork of a painting, or of the surface quality of a sculpture, rather than providing for an overall impression.

In other cases, lighting may be part of the setting, and this can involve some difficult lighting issues. For example, if a setting is to be seen by candlelight, the candles must be visible, but it is quite impossible for a museum to have candles actually burning in the display. Electric simulations are available and can appear surprisingly realistic, but it is a salutary lesson to learn just how little light a candle emits. The problem is that to boost the output of the electric candle would destroy the illusion, and to increase the illumination by means of concealed electric lamps would seem to defeat at least one aspect of the educational purpose. The reality is that authenticity can conflict with needs for effective display.

For the lighting designer to establish a distinct and recognizable style

Lighting designers are becoming increasingly recognized as professional contributors to the design process, particularly in theatre and other entertainment industries. Some top-name designers have made significant reputations for their specialized work in museum lighting, and perhaps we will see the emergence of recognizable styles associated with individual lighting designers. After all, there are some well-known museums around the world where architects have made distinct personal statements, so why should not lighting designers make their own individual marks through the unique style of their work?

The approach taken in this book is that as artists create their works, they impart to them certain visible attributes. The lighting designer's prime task is to reveal those attributes in ways that meet the expectations of the viewers. This implies that the visual qualities of the lighting are to be determined by the nature of the art, subject as always to practical constraints such as conservation. A designer who brings preconceived notions of lighting to the design process is seeking to impose upon the viewer's experience, and this is not in accord with the approach taken in this book.

Towards a lighting design philosophy. . .

The purpose of this short chapter is to explore some of the issues pertaining to the provision of lighting in museums in general, and for the presentation of art in particular. However, it should be expected that a personal design philosophy will evolve with practice. For a dedicated museum lighting designer, it is necessary to continually question that philosophy and to reassesses the principles on which it is based.

Revealing visual attributes　　2

An artwork may be regarded as an artefact that has been crafted to interact with light. An artist who applies paint to canvas is adding pigments, which are substances that have the property to absorb select bands of the spectrum of incident light, and in this way to modify the spectrum of reflected light. There are techniques of application to further modify interactions with light, such as impasto, which gives texture to the paint layer, and the addition of glaze to the paint surface to affect how light is scattered upon incidence. In another medium, the reason why sculptors have such reverence for marble is because of the range of control that it enables them to have over how light is reflected at the surface. Roughly tooled, marble has a textured opaque surface that can generate strong light and shade patterns. It can be smoothed to a diffusing surface that gives softly graded shading patterns, or it can be polished to an opalescent surface that shows specularly reflected highlights. The long periods of studio work that art students undergo are largely concerned with developing the skill to manage their chosen medium and to control its interactions with light. For artworks to be effectively displayed, the lighting must have the potential to reveal the visual attributes upon which the artwork depends. Lighting for art requires a lighting designer who has understanding of art media and how its interactions with light enable visual attributes to be revealed.

This chapter deals with the physical nature of light, the human visual response, and ways in which visual attributes of objects may be revealed by light.

Light and illumination

Light is a flow of photons, where a photon is an elementary particle of radiant energy. In a vacuum, all photons travel at the same velocity, this being the great universal constant that is the speed of light, and there is a vibration associated with their movement. This rate of vibration can vary over a vast range, and this difference causes photons to have very different properties. Back in the late nineteenth century, scientists learned how to

Facing page: *Huntington Gallery, San Marino, California*

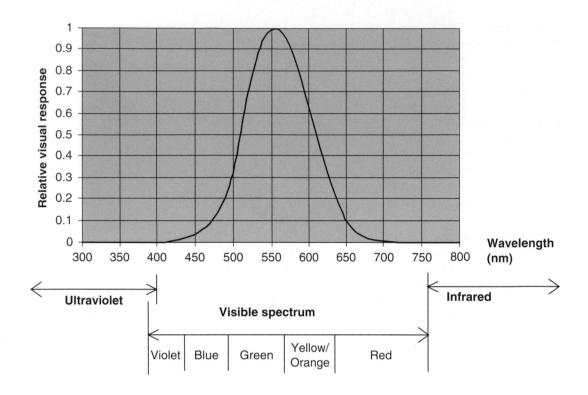

Figure 2.1: *Human visual response to radiant power according to wavelength*

measure wavelengths due to this vibration with high levels of accuracy, and this has led to different types of radiation being classified into wavelength bands. The visible spectrum is the waveband of radiation for which, when focused upon the retina, the absorbed energy of the photons stimulates the retinal photoreceptors and causes a sensory response in the visual cortex of the brain. This is the property that distinguishes light from all other types of radiation, and it is a very narrow wavelength band. It covers just one octave, ranging from 380 to 760 nanometres (nm), where one nanometre is one millionth of a millimetre (Figure 2.1). The adjacent wavebands are infrared (IR) and ultraviolet (UV), and there is more to be said about these non-visible wavebands in the following chapter.

Lumens and illuminance

The visible waveband can be displayed by passing a beam of broad-spectrum 'white' light through a prism or reflecting it from a diffraction grating, and the pure spectral colours indicated in Figure 2.1 will be evident. It may be observed that the colours do not appear equally bright, but rather the mid-part of the waveband is noticeably brightest, and the colours fade away in both directions. The bell-shaped curve shown in Figure 2.1 has been established by research employing normal-sighted human observers, and represents a typical visual response for an observer who is photopically (see following section) adapted. When light is incident on a surface, the density of radiant power may be measured in watts per square metre (W/m^2), and this is a purely physical quantity. Alternatively, it may be measured with an instrument that evaluates the radiation at each wavelength according to the typical visual response indicated in the figure. In this case, the radiant power is evaluated as lumens, and the density of incident lumens is given in lux (lx), where one lux equals one lumen per square metre. In this way, instead of being a physical quantity, the lumen is a psychophysical quantity. The typical visual response has been defined by an international standard since 1924, so that a lux is a lux no matter where in the world you are or who is the observer. The curve in Figure 2.1 is referred to as the V(λ) curve, as V is the symbol for visual response, and the curve expresses this response as a function of wavelength, indicated by the symbol λ. However, people who are colour blind, or more accurately colour defective, have a response to light that differs from V(λ).

Reflectance

As explained, an incident light density of one lumen per square metre equals one lux, and this is the unit of illuminance. The ratio of reflected light to incident light is the reflectance of a surface, which may be expressed as a percentage (0 to 100 per cent) or as a factor (0 to 1.0). Do not be confused by supposing that surfaces have to be shiny to have high reflectance. Fresh matt white paint may have a reflectance of 0.95, although a white painted wall is not likely to have a maintained reflectance higher than 0.8. Another source of confusion is to suppose that what we assess to be a mid-lightness colour will have a reflectance around 0.5, whereas it is more likely to be around 0.2. Some paint manufacturers give reflectance values on their paint charts, and it is an instructive process to try matching the colours on one of these charts to actual room surfaces. As will be discussed, room surface reflectance values are important factors in lighting design.

Exitance

As illuminance (E) is the measure of light incident on a surface, the measure of light exiting from a surface is exitance (M). This term may take account of reflected light, transmitted light, or light emitted by a self-luminous material. For opaque, non-luminous

Figure 2.2: *The basic terminology*
of lighting

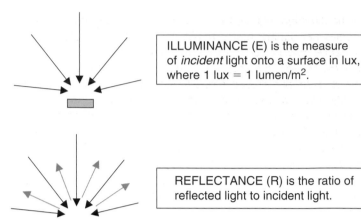

ILLUMINANCE (E) is the measure of *incident* light onto a surface in lux, where 1 lux = 1 lumen/m².

REFLECTANCE (R) is the ratio of reflected light to incident light.

EXITANCE (M) is the measure of light *exiting* the surface in lumens/m². For any opaque surface, $M = E \times R$ lm/m². Exitance also accounts for light from transparent or self-luminous materials. If the exiting light is perfectly diffused, then LUMINANCE (L)= M/π cd/m², otherwise luminance applies only for a specific direction of view.

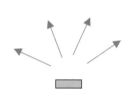

materials, illuminance and exitance are related by the expression $M = E \times R$, where R is reflectance expressed as a factor (Figure 2.2). It should be noted that the lux unit is used only for incident light, and exitance is expressed in lumens per square metre (lm/m²). As well as using these measures for illuminated surfaces, they may be applied for measuring light at the eye. It is common practice in museum galleries to measure light incident on displayed objects in lux, and hand-held luxmeters that are calibrated for the typical visual response are available from specialist stores. Less common practice, but very informative, is using a luxmeter to measure light incident at the eye of a viewer in lux, which equals the average exitance of the field of view in lm/m². This is discussed in the next section as well as in following chapters.

Luminance

There is another more specialized lighting measurement that deals with light from different elements within the field of view, and this is luminance. It defines the luminous intensity of an element in a specific direction relative to its projected area in that direction, in candelas per square metre (cd/m^2). For opaque matt surfaces, luminance may be related to illuminance by the expression $L = E \times R/\pi$, but for anything other than an illuminated matt surface there is no simple relationship. The luminance meter incorporates an optical system so that when the operator holds the instrument at his or her eye and directs it towards the element to be measured, light from that element is focused onto the instrument's photocell. In this way, a luminance value is viewpoint-specific, and for glossy surfaces luminance can change dramatically with small changes in viewing position. It does, however, enable precise evaluation of contrast, such as the contrast between a displayed object and the background against which it is seen, or between a typeface and the paper on which it is printed. It is not uncommon for luminance to be loosely applied to describing situations that are not viewpoint-specific, and for which it would be more correct and a lot more simple to use exitance.

Human response to light

Adaptation

Human vision operates over a huge range of available light. From clear sky summer sunlight to moonless starlight we can see our surroundings, albeit with differing levels of effectiveness, and this is a range of ambient light levels of around ten million to one. To enable us to cope with this range, our eyes have two overlapping but largely independent visual systems. The photoreceptors in our retinas are of two distinct types: the rods and the cones. The rods are more sensitive and greatly outnumber the cones, and they are all of the same type. The cones are of three types, and they are very unevenly spread over the retina. Despite these differences, all of the receptors work in the same way. They generate photo-pigment at their light-responsive regions, and these pigments absorb photons from specific wavebands of the visible spectrum. The absorbed energy stimulates the receptor, causing an impulse to the sensory system, and at the same time it causes bleaching, which has the effect of reducing the absorbing power of the pig-ment. As light levels reduce, the rate of regeneration of the photopigments exceeds the rate of bleaching, causing the sensi-tivity of the receptors to increase. Under steady conditions, regeneration and bleaching fall into equilibrium. In this way, the photoreceptors adapt their sensitivity to prevailing light levels, enabling detection of relatively small luminance contrasts in the field of view. Over an extensive range, it is this process of adaptation that ensures that, as museum visitors move into zones of substantially

Table 2.1 *Visual adaptation ranges*

Adaptation range	Luminance (cd/m²)	Exitance (lm/m²)
Photopic	>3	>10
Mesopic	0.001 to 3	0.003 to 10
Scotopic	<0.001	<0.003

decreasing light levels, they suffer only a much more gradual loss of ability to discriminate detail and colour.

Adaptation does not happen instantly, nor does it operate without variation over the whole range ambient light levels. There are three distinct ranges within the field of visual adaptation, shown in Table 2.1.

When vision is adapted within the scotopic range, the radiant power onto the retina is insufficient to stimulate the cone receptors and vision is entirely dependent on the rods. It can take a young person up to 40 minutes to fully adapt to very low light levels in this range, at which time regeneration of photopigment is complete and the rods have their maximum sensitivity. Because all rods have the same photopigment, there is no colour discrimination and vision is restricted to brightness differences. Resolution is poor, for although there are 120 million rod receptors in each retina, over much of the retina they are connected in groups to the neural pathways, sacrificing resolution for sensitivity. More significantly, they are totally absent from the central area of the retina, making it impossible to fixate upon a small area of interest.

Within the mesopic range both rods and cones are operative, with the cones becoming increasingly active and the rods increasingly inactive as the light level increases. When the luminance of the field of view has a value of 3 cd/m² or more, which is roughly equivalent to an exitance of 10 lm/m² or more, the rods are completely overwhelmed and vision is entirely due to cone responses. While adaptation occurs much more quickly within the photopic range, generally it takes longer to adapt to reducing light levels than to increasing levels, and the process operates more slowly for older viewers.

Discrimination of detail

The non-uniformity of the distribution of photoreceptors in the retina has been mentioned, and this significantly affects vision. The rods, which greatly outnumber the cones, are broadly spread over the retina except that they are entirely absent from the small central area, the fovea centralis. This area is reserved for cones, which are packed in at a density of 150 000 per square millimetre, whereas over the rest of the retina the density of cones is less than 10 000/mm^2. This explains much of how vision works under photopic conditions. The eyes must not be thought of as picture-making devices, like digital cameras, but instead they are instruments of search. Together they cover slightly more than 180 degrees in the horizontal plane, albeit with low resolution. When an event catches the attention, the head turns and the eyes fixate, that is to say, each eye aligns to focus the zone of interest onto its fovea. The muscles that rotate the eyes in their sockets cause the eyes to undergo a series of rapid movements, referred to as saccadic movements, resulting in the zone being scanned by the fovea. This is the process that enables us to quickly form a general impression of an unfamiliar environment, to direct our attention to items of interest, and to examine these at high resolution. Phototropism is the tendency for our attention to be drawn by the brightest elements in the field of view.

The ability of human vision to detect fine detail is termed visual acuity, and there is a large body of literature on this topic. Generally acuity increases as light levels increase up to very high levels, so that where there is a need to maximize acuity, as for example for picture restoration, high illuminance levels have to be provided. From this high level, acuity declines gradually as the light level is reduced until the threshold of the mesopic adaptation range is encountered, at which point acuity declines rapidly. As we fixate on an item of interest at this lower light level, the radiant power focused onto the fovea is insufficient to adequately stimulate the densely packed cones. Where the need is to provide for an adequate level of acuity with minimum light exposure of the object, an illuminance that provides for visual adaptation that just exceeds the photopic/mesopic threshold should be the objective. This is discussed further in the following chapter.

To maximize the visibility of detail, luminance values surrounding the detail on which the viewer is fixating should not exceed the luminance of the detail. As shown in Figure 2.3, a luminaire within the viewer's field of view may be a source of direct glare, or more commonly in the museum context, glare may occur due to the reflected image of a luminaire, particularly if it appears adjacent to the displayed object. Glare affects viewers adversely in two distinct ways. The human eye is an imperfect optical instrument, and some of the light entering the eye is scattered as it passes through the transparent media that fill the eye. When we fixate onto an item of interest, light entering the eye from other parts of the field

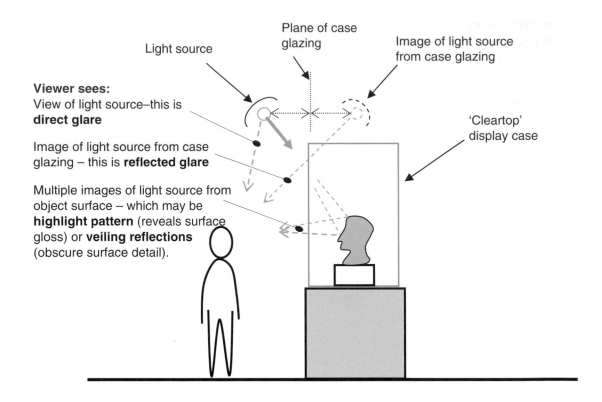

Plane of case
glazing

Light source

Image of light source
from case glazing

Viewer sees:
View of light source–this is
direct glare

'Cleartop'
display case

Image of light source from case
glazing – this is **reflected glare**

Multiple images of light source from
object surface – which may be
highlight pattern (reveals surface
gloss) or **veiling reflections**
(obscure surface detail).

Figure 2.3: *Light arriving at a museum viewer's eyes*

of view makes no contribution to the information that we are searching for, but adds to the veil of scattered light within the eye, reducing the visibility of the item of interest. This is disability glare, and its effect increases with age as the optical media lose their clarity. At the same time, the viewer's attention is attracted towards the brightest element in the field of view, and particularly where the glare source or its image appears close to the item of interest, the result is discomfort glare. For either type of glare the cause is much the same, and the cure usually becomes obvious if a simple diagram of the sort shown in Figure 2.3 is constructed.

Figure 2.3 also shows a specular reflection of the light source being directed towards the viewer from the surface of the object, and whether or not this is a problem depends upon the object attributes that the viewer is seeking to see. Reflected highlights are crucial for revealing surface qualities such as gloss, sheen and lustre, but where they occur, they obscure detail such as surface colour or text. Large sources, which means sources which have large angular subtense at the object, may reduce the visibility of detail by casting a luminous veil over part or all of the object's surface. Such veiling reflections can cause significant visibility problems, particularly if they are so widespread that viewers are unable to avoid their effect by adjusting their viewing positions. Veiling reflections caused by small sources are more easily avoided by head movement, and may produce attractive highlight patterns on objects that have appropriate characteristics.

To avoid the likelihood of reflected glare occurring in the immediate surround to the display object it is only necessary to ensure matt surfaces for the supporting materials, and a can of dulling spray can be a useful tool for achieving this. It is not necessary to display objects against dark backgrounds. While there are situations in which high object/background contrasts can catch attention and provide a stimulating appearance, this is not a formula for success as repetition can lead quickly to a sense of discomfort and visual overload. It is necessary to distinguish between contrasts which reveal fine detail in the displayed objects, and contrasts between the objects and their surroundings.

Colour vision

The seven million cones in the retina are of three different types, according to their photopigments. These pigments have maximum absorption in different zones of the visible spectrum, and are best classified as long, medium and short wavelength cones (L-, M- and S-cones) although they often are referred to as the red, green and blue cones. This is misleading because they would not appear to have these colours, as these terms refer to the spectral components that they absorb rather than those they reflect. Our ability to experience colour is entirely due to differentials in stimulation of these three cone types, and it might be supposed that the colour perceived would be determined by their proportional responses. Recent research has shown that this is not the case, and interestingly, this research has confirmed observations dating back more than one hundred years. It had been pointed out that the spectrum does not appear to be a continuous transition, but that within the range of spectral colours there are some clear and distinct hues separated by zones which appear to be mixtures of these hues. The four 'pure' hues are red, yellow, green and blue, and only certain mixtures are possible. For example, yellowish-reds and bluish-reds are possible, but greenish reds are not, and this led to an opponent-colours theory which seemed for some while to be in direct opposition to the established principles of trichromacy.

Figure 2.4: *The three retinal cone types and the visual response channels, comprising an achromatic non-opponent channel and two chromatic opponent channels*

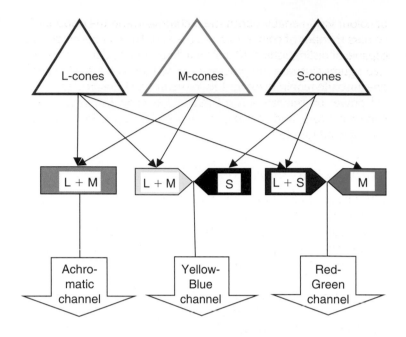

Figure 2.5: *Schematic illustration of the channel responses for the two chromatic opponent channels*

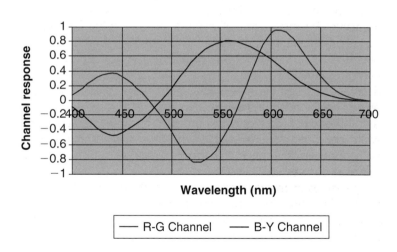

Figure 2.4 shows the responses of the three retinal cone types feeding into three channels which convey information to the visual cortex of the brain. The achromatic channel signals the level of stimulation at a given zone of the retina, which is represented by the sum of responses of the L- and M-cones and may be seen as a luminance response. The two chromatic channels are opponent channels, and signal the balance of yellow-blue and red-green responses as illustrated in Figure 2.5. Figure 2.4 indicates the connections of cone responses which provide the inputs to the channels, and this quite recent understanding of the process

of colour vision enables both the trichromatic and the opponent-colours theories of colour vision to co-exist. Human observers are capable of distinguishing 10 million differences of colour, and these two figures illustrate the process by which this is done. However, one absolute requirement for this to occur is that the incident radiant power on the retina is sufficient to effectively stimulate the cone receptors, and that means that the viewer is in a state of photopic adaptation.

Colour characteristics of lighting

While coloured lighting is often used for decorative purposes, it has no part to play where the aim is to illuminate objects so that their chromatic attributes can be appreciated. For this, the two lighting concepts that are used to describe the colour properties of lighting are colour temperature and colour rendering.

There are many varieties of 'white' light, and it is a peculiarity of human preference that while we readily accept a range from bluish-white (which we describe as 'cool') to yellowish- or even orangish-white (which we describe as 'warm'), we do not accept greenish-white or mauvish-white light as appearing natural or attractive. For this reason, all of the light sources that are offered for general lighting purposes may be classified as either warm, intermediate, or cool, and that offers a simple description of the overall colour cast of the lighting. Colour temperature takes this definition a stage further. It is common experience that metal objects can be heated to become luminous; at first the appearance is dull cherry red, then glowing orange-red, and eventually bright white-hot. Scientists employ the concept of a hypothetical 'black body' for which the spectrum of emitted radiation at any temperature can be predicted, even at temperatures above the melting temperatures of metals, and those at which the black body may become blue-hot. The kelvin absolute temperature scale is used to define colour temperature, so that as temperature increases, the colour appearance of emitted light changes from warm to intermediate to cool. Any nominally 'white' light source can be accorded a correlated colour temperature (CCT), which is the absolute temperature of a black body when its emitted light most closely matches the colour appearance of the light source. It does not mean that any part of the light source is actually operating at that temperature, it is simply a way of describing the colour appearance of the emitted light. Within the CCT range 3300 to 5000K, the colour appearance of lighting may be described as 'intermediate', so that light from lamps having CCT values less than 3300K tend to give a 'warm' or yellowish cast to the spaces that they illuminate, and lamps having CCT 5000K or more give a 'cool' or bluish cast. It should not be supposed that there is a sudden switch at these two temperatures, but rather CCT is a continuous scale with a neutral zone, above which colour appearance is increasingly 'cool' and below which it is increasingly 'warm'. For indoor lighting, it appears as an overall cast which affects the appearance of all coloured surfaces and objects, including neutral or achromatic (i.e. white, light grey, dark grey) materials.

Colour rendering concerns the effect of lighting on the appearance of chromatic (i.e. having hue) surfaces. Previously adaptation was considered with regard to the luminance of the visual field, but chromatic adaptation also occurs and to some extent it overcomes effects of colour temperature. If we switch on an incandescent lamp with a CCT of 2700K in a daylit room, the emitted light has a distinctly yellowish appearance. However, if we return to that same room at night when the whole space is lit by incandescent lamps, we may be conscious that the lighting has a 'warm' appearance, but it will not appear distinctly yellow. The difference is our state of chromatic adaptation, and our notion of what is a natural appearance for all of the objects around us is affected by the colour characteristics of the light to which we are adapted.

The CIE (International Commission on Illumination) published a procedure in 1965 for specifying the Colour Rendering Index (CRI) of a light source. Its scale is simplicity itself: a lamp is given a score out of 100. Colour rendering is, however, a complex phenomenon and the rendering properties of a lamp cannot be defined adequately in such a simple way. The procedure for determining the index is certainly not simple, but as this is an issue that demands the attention of museum staff who are concerned with lighting, it is necessary to have some understanding of what the index stands for. A test source is compared with a reference source, this being a black body at the temperature equal to the CCT of the test source. (If the CCT is 5000K or more, the reference source becomes a standard daylight spectral power distribution.) The colour appearances of the reference and test sources are determined by calculating their chromaticity values, which enable them to be defined in a specified colour space, and an adaptation allowance is made for any difference between their chromaticity values. The CIE has specified eight test colour samples in terms of their spectral reflectance distributions, which range all round the hue circle and are of moderate saturation, enabling calculation of their chromaticity values when illuminated by either source. If the chromaticity values for all eight test colour samples under the test source exactly match those under the reference source, the test source is accorded a CRI of 100. Otherwise, all differences are summed, and from this a CRI is calculated, so that a lower CRI value indicates a greater sum of differences in test colour sample chromaticity values between the test source and its reference source.

The CIE has specified a series of colour rendering groups, and the highest of these, Group 1A, is restricted to CRI values not less than 90, and it may be recommended that all lamps used in museums and art galleries should be within this group. It is, however, very important that CCT values are also taken into account. The CRI system depends on viewers being fully adapted to the light source, so that if all light sources are closely matched for CCT and all of them have CRI values in the 90s; then it may be expected that appearance of coloured materials will seem natural. The overall colour appearance of the illumination will depend on the CCT, and the levels of detail and colour discrimination will depend on the light level. The interactive nature of these metrics needs to be understood whenever they are to be used for specifying lighting conditions.

Situations occur in which it is not practical or even possible to ensure close matching of CCT. An example of this is a daylit gallery in which display lighting is to be used during daylight hours. If a high CCT is chosen for the display lighting to match the daylight, then it probably will not match the night-time general illumination, and vice versa. This means that for at least some of the time, the display lighting will appear to give a colour cast to achromatic materials, and may also give an unnatural appearance to chromatic materials.

Also, situations may occur when lamps of suitable dimensions or light outputs are not available with CRI values in the 90s, and a lamp of lower CRI has to be used. It is in these circumstances that the limitations of CRI become apparent. A CRI less than 90 means that differences in colour rendering compared with the reference source probably would be visible, but no indication is given as to the nature of these differences and whether they would be a problem in a particular application. The CRI calculation treats all differences as if they are equally detrimental, so that a lamp that makes greens appear slightly yellowish- or bluish-green is rated down in the same way as if it made them appear slightly pale green, or more strongly green. The conclusion has to be that this colour metric must be treated with caution, and that the only way to be sure that the appearance of coloured materials will be entirely satisfactory is by trial and critical observation.

Ageing and visual defects

The codes and standards that provide guidance for general lighting practice are based on data gathered from human subjects, who generally have been healthy young people with normal vision. Among museum visitors, there can be no doubt that such people are able to enjoy clearer, sharper and more colourful visual experiences than older viewers. Light arriving at the eye has to pass through layers of transparent media to reach the photoreceptors at the back of the retina, and these media lose their clarity over time. Compared with a 20-year-old, only half as much light reaches the retina at age 50, and this reduces to one third at age 65. Unfortunately, that is not the full extent of deterioration of visual ability that afflicts the aged. A few studies of effects of age on work performance have been reported, but a study by Knoblauch et al. (1997) is particularly relevant to museum lighting as it examined effects of age and illuminance on colour discrimination ability.

The Farnsworth–Munsell 100-hue test of colour discrimination ability presents a subject with a jumbled assortment of coloured discs. For example, these might all be basically green, but differing in hue between yellow-green and blue-green. The subject has to arrange the discs in sequence. The hue steps are small, so that even young people in ample illumination are likely to make a few mistakes. When finished, the experimenter determines a test score that takes account of both the number and magnitude of incorrect placements.

Seventy-five colour-normal viewers in the range 20 to 78 years old completed the test under illuminances ranging from 5.7 to 1800 lux, and the results are plotted in Figure 2.6. It should be noted that increasing test score indicates increasing error rate. The researchers comment, '...it seems that the effects of ageing are similar to the effects of lower illuminance level...' At a given illuminance, the effect of age on test score can be read off, or to achieve a given test score, the illuminance required by each age group can be read off.

The initial question is, what test score corresponds to satisfactory viewing in a museum context? For people with healthy vision, the onset of noticeable change in their vision often occurs in their mid-forties. If we hypothesize that the 40–49 years group find 50 lux satisfactory, this corresponds to a test score of 0.77. To maintain this performance requires 130 lux for the 50–59 years group, 300 lux for the 60–69 years group, and 900 lux for the 70–79 years group. Meanwhile, the 20–29 group require only 12 lux.

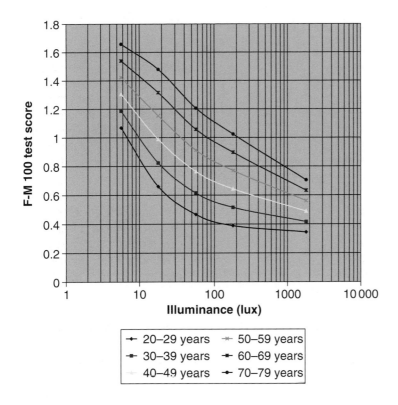

Figure 2.6: *Age and illuminance effects on colour discrimination performance. After Knoblauch et al. (1997)*

Legend:
- 20–29 years
- 30–39 years
- 40–49 years
- 50–59 years
- 60–69 years
- 70–79 years

Obviously, it would be impractical, and probably impossible, to provide elderly viewers with visual experiences that match those of young viewers. We have to note that at every illuminance, the young groups achieve higher test scores, and we may presume from this that they are enjoying richer visual experiences when they visit art galleries than their seniors. The effects of ageing occur gradually, and it is probable that people become accustomed to this change and, as time goes by, do not notice their loss until they are confronted with a viewing situation that fails to satisfy. While some illuminance increase might alleviate their current situation, we should not suppose that it would be possible, let alone practical, to fully restore their viewing experience through illumination.

Figure 2.6 throws some light on differences in the ways that ageing affects vision. At the highest illuminance, all groups perform best and the range of scores is least. As illuminance is reduced, the younger groups maintain high performance until illuminance drops to around 50 lux, at which point deterioration becomes more rapid as adaptation falls below the photopic range and cone vision starts to fail. However, for the older groups, deterioration commences progressively as illuminance drops below 1800 lux, and at around 50 lux the range of scores is at its greatest. In other words, at around this level, the prospects for compensating ageing with increased illuminance would seem to be at their least.

These data on the effects of ageing refer to healthy people with normal vision for their age. It has to be assumed that people who have visual defects that can be corrected by wearing spectacles will be so equipped, but that leaves many whose capacity to enjoy a museum visit is compromised. Not all visual defects are ameliorated by increased illuminance, but it can be said with confidence that all groups who have seeing difficulties will benefit from rigorous elimination of glare. Some will want to approach close to the displayed objects, and this can create problems for other viewers as well as security staff. It can be helpful to have captions and other written material mounted so that visitors are able to read them at close range, perhaps by mounting them on any barriers that may be installed to ensure that visitors keep their distance. Contrast is every bit as important as font size for visibility of these captions, so that while similarly toned text and background may give the caption boards an attractive appearance, they are likely to cause difficulties for the visually impaired.

Apart from viewing the exhibits, it is necessary also to be aware of difficulties that people with visual defects may encounter in moving through a museum, particularly where low ambient light levels are provided for conservation reasons. Abrupt transitions to dim lighting can cause significant loss of vision that may persist for several seconds, particularly for elderly people who are slow to adapt. Even when adaptation is complete, difficulties are likely to persist in situations where low reflectances are used to keep ambient light levels down. Light-coloured strips should be used to identify obstructions, and for floor markings indicating changes of direction or level. Low-mounted luminaires should be added wherever shadows make the light-coloured strips appear dim.

Light levels in museums

Researchers at the Bartlett School of Architecture and Planning, London, have examined people's responses to lighting in a mock-up art gallery (Loe et al., 1982). Subjects completed semantic differential questionnaires to give their assessments of the appearance of five framed paintings, and of the overall space, under several different types of lighting at six different light levels: 10, 25, 50, 100, 200 and 400 lux. The researchers were concerned about

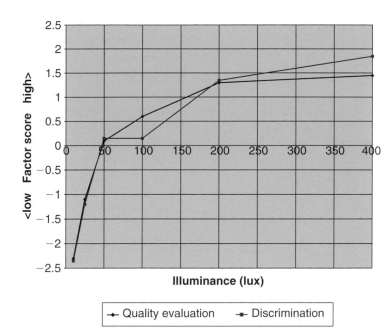

Figure 2.7: *Subjective assessment ratings for the appearance of paintings viewed under daylight in a simulated art gallery (after Loe et al., 1982)*

colour rendering and included three types of fluorescent lamps, all of which are now obsolete, and fortunately they also included daylight. The questionnaire results were subjected to factor analysis to identify the principal dimensions by which the subjects differentiated the lighting conditions, and two significant factors emerged. The first was a Discrimination Factor, as it related to ability to discriminate detail and colour and to provide bright, clear impressions of the paintings. The second was a Quality Evaluation Factor, as it related to the degree of pleasure derived from viewing the pictures, and was associated with terms such as pleasant, attractive and stimulating. The mean scores of these factors for viewing the paintings under daylight are shown relative to illuminance in Figure 2.7.

It can be seen that 50 lux is the lowest light level that provided satisfactory viewing in the test situation, and that for the illuminance values below this level, satisfaction plummeted. This is to be expected from the foregoing discussion. Increasing the light level above 50 lux gave increased satisfaction up to the 200 lux level, above which satisfaction increases were only slight. Although discrimination and overall quality emerged from the analysis as two distinct factors, their scores are closely in agreement and lead to the broad conclusions that a light level of 50 lux is necessary for satisfactory viewing, but where it is acceptable to provide a higher illuminance, viewers will prefer 200 lux. There was found to be little benefit to be gained from increasing illuminance up to 400 lux.

It may be noted that the 24 subjects who took part in this experiment comprised equal numbers of males and females, with ages ranging from late teens to early fifties, and all subjects were checked for normal colour vision. The relevance of the findings from this study to conservation concerns is discussed in the following chapter.

Revealing with light

Whenever lighting is applied to a museum object, it is necessary that consideration is given to the visual attributes of the object that are to be revealed, for this determines the characteristics of the lighting that are appropriate.

Surface attributes

When a ray of light is incident on the surface of an opaque material, some of the light is reflected and some is absorbed, so that $\rho + \alpha = 1.0$, where ρ and α are reflectance and absorptance respectively. It is the reflected component that provides us with visual information about the material and the object of which it is part, but there are two distinctly different processes by which reflection may occur, and they affect substantially the appearance of the illuminated surface.

As has been discussed, light is a flow of photons, where photons are primary energy particles. Solid materials comprise molecules locked into a matrix in which there is space between individual molecules, allowing photons arriving at the boundary of a solid material to pass between the molecules and into the surface layer of the substance. Some of the photons are absorbed by the molecules, but others may undergo multiple reflections to re-emerge from the surface. The proportion of incident light that undergoes this back-scattering process is re-emitted from the surface as diffusely reflected light, as illustrated in Figure 2.8, which has a spherical cosine spatial distribution regardless of the directional nature of the incident light. In this way, the intensity of reflected light from a surface element in any direction bears a constant relationship to the projected area of the element in that direction, so that is has the same luminance from all directions of view. This is a property of a perfectly matt or diffusing surface.

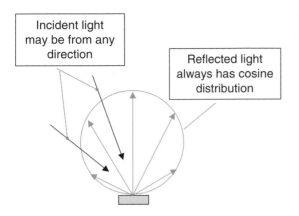

Figure 2.8: *Diffuse reflection, otherwise known as isotropic re-emission*

Incident light may be from any direction

Reflected light always has cosine distribution

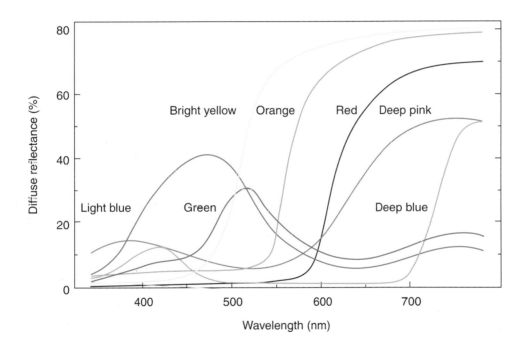

Not only may the spatial distribution of the diffusely reflected light be very different from that of the incident light, but also its spectral distribution. Pigments are materials chosen for their ability to absorb light at specific wavelengths and to reflect it at others. The more saturated their colours, the more wavelength-selective is the absorption process. Figure 2.9 illustrates some typical spectral reflectance curves, and it is the spectral re-shaping of incident 'white' light that enables us to describe pigments in terms of their characteristic colours. To distinguish the characteristics of this type of reflection, it may be referred to as isotropic re-emission, and

Figure 2.9: *Typical pigment spectral reflectance curves (with permission CIBSE, London)*

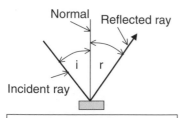

- the angle of incidence i
  equals the angle of
  reflection r.
- the incident ray, the
  normal and the reflected
  ray lie in the same plane.

Figure 2.10: *Specular, or regular, reflection*

a surface that produces only this type of reflection would be described as perfectly matt, without any gloss or sheen.

The other type of reflection that concerns us is generally referred to as specular reflection, and for a plane surface specular reflection complies with the principles of regular reflection as illustrated in Figure 2.10. This type of reflection may come about in one of two ways. Light incident on a smooth electroconductive surface undergoes reflection without photons entering the surface, and if reflectance is high at all visible wavelengths, we have a mirror. Polished metals that act as full mirrors include silver, aluminium and chromium. Some metals have lower reflectance at shorter wavelengths and impart a distinctive colour to reflected light, and in order of increasing effect, these include gold, brass and copper. The other way in which specular reflection may occur is when light is incident on the surface of a liquid or a liquid-state material, in which case some of the light enters and may be transmitted through the material, but a portion undergoes regular reflection at the surface. Clear liquids such as water demonstrate these properties well, which occur because the molecules are not tightly bound into a matrix but are loosely tied by elastic bonds that permit photons to pass through the material, albeit with reduced velocity. There are some materials which, when they cool from a liquid state, become so viscous that they assume the rigid cohesion of a solid-state material without losing the molecular structure of a liquid. Glass and clear plastics may be referred to as either super-cooled liquids or amorphous solids, as they possess both the transparency of liquids and the rigidity of solids. Other examples include clear varnishes, lacquers and glazes, and even wax polishes. These materials transform the surface optical properties of the materials onto which they are applied, presenting to the viewer a distribution of reflected light that is distinctly different from diffusely reflected light.

The two important differences from diffuse reflection are that the spatial distribution of reflected light is highly dependent on the spatial distribution of incident light, and the spectral distribution of reflected light is highly dependent on the spectral distribution of the light source. Figure 2.10 illustrates specular reflection at a smooth surface, which may apply to polished metal surfaces and to air/liquid surfaces. However, a stippled or satin finish surface will produce a spread or even a diffused distribution from a single incident ray, but the colour characteristics of the reflected light will be those of the source, perhaps modified by a metallic hue, and not those of the underlying material. A light source that encloses a substantial solid angle at the surface will also produce a spread reflection, and an area source that effectively surrounds the surface will produce a diffused distribution of reflected light regardless of the smoothness of the surface. Again, it is the colour characteristics of this reflected light that distinguish it from diffusely reflected light, and it may be noted that although isotropic re-emission is an ungainly mouthful, it does describe very succinctly the distinct nature of the diffuse reflection process.

The reason for this discussion of reflection is that, more often than not, the visual presentation of museum exhibits depends upon surface attributes being revealed by reflected light. This is not always the case and transmitted and refracted light will be discussed in the following section, but more often than not the image of the exhibit that is focused onto the viewer's retina comprises light that has been reflected from the object's surface, some by diffuse and some by specular reflection. The information imparted by these two types of reflection are quite different, and for successful lighting it is essential that the designer has given thoughtful consideration to what are the surface attributes that are to be revealed. Is it the three-dimensional form of the object or the texture of its surface? Is it surface colour or fine surface detail? Is it the gloss or the sheen, or matt nature of the surface? The directional balance of the lighting is all-important for achieving the balance of diffuse and specular reflection that will reveal the chosen attributes.

The three lighting patterns

When a three-dimensional object intercepts a directional flow of light, three distinct lighting patterns may be generated. They are:

- the shading pattern, being a variation of surface exitance due to changing incidence of light in response to the object's surface form

- the highlight pattern, being specularly reflected images of light sources distorted by the object's surface form (or for transparent materials, due to internally reflected images)

- the shadow pattern, being shadows cast by convex surface elements onto other parts of the object's surface, or onto other adjacent surfaces.

The appearance of these lighting patterns crucially affects the appearance of an object and recognition of object attributes, as illustrated in Figure 2.11 (a–d). The obvious difference in object attributes is that the two rear dish and spoon sets are black and the front pair is white. Closer inspection shows that for each pair, the left set is glossy and the right set is matt.

2.11a

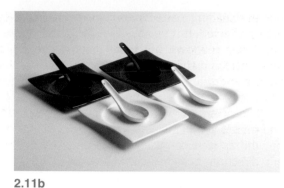

2.11b

2.11c

2.11d

Figure 2.11: *Effects of lighting upon the appearance of a group of four objects: two black and two white, and two glossy and two matt. (a) Thoroughly diffused overhead illumination. (b) Flow of light from right, due to a large diffusing light source. (c) Flow of light from right, due to a compact, directional light source. (d) Multiple compact sources*

Lighting condition (a) is overhead and thoroughly diffused, and may be thought of as the indoor equivalent of an overcast sky. The only set to show any appreciable response to this situation is the glossy black set. The glossy white set must generate a similar specularly reflected pattern, but it is almost indistinguishable against its white surface. It appears dull, as do the two matt sets.

Lighting condition (b) adds the flow of light due to a diffusing light source. The actual source was what photographers call a 'soft box', and may be thought of as the effect of sunlight or spotlighting reflected from a light-coloured wall, or a patch of sky visible through a window. The two white sets have responded strongly, and the curved surface forms of the dishes are clearly revealed by distinctive shading patterns, but the appearance of the two black sets have hardly changed.

Lighting condition (c) produces a similar direction of flow to (b), but now the lighting has 'sharpness'. The 'soft box' has been replaced by a compact spotlight, and the effect is like sunshine breaking through the clouds. The appearance of the two white sets is dominated by dense and sharply defined shadow patterns, but the shading patterns and the modelling they produce are hardly affected. It is obvious that the black spoons must be casting similar shadows, but these shadow patterns are barely evident. Instead highlight patterns dominate on the black sets, being intense and sharply defined for the glossy set and spread and diffused for the matt set. Although the lighting patterns appear distinctly different on both the black and white pairs and the glossy and matt pairs, the overall scene has coherence in that the 'flow of light' appears consistent throughout in terms of both strength and direction.

Lighting condition (d) is produced by multiple compact sources, and may be likened to the effect of a jeweller's shop window. There is a multiplicity of criss-crossing shadows, which although sharply defined, lack density. Highlights are apparent, particularly where curvatures are sharp so that small areas of surface gather specular images over wide angles. The glossy black set in particular shows this effect, but overall, the scene lacks a coherent flow of light.

The foregoing comments relate to opaque objects, and some differences occur when we apply similar observations to transparent objects, as shown in Figure 2.12 (a–e).

In this case, lighting condition (a) is achieved by a trans-illuminated background. This is a popular way of displaying glass objects in museums, as it is effective for showing colour or other qualities within the substance of the glass. While the clarity of this cut crystal bowl is well revealed, its decorative features are obscure.

Lighting condition (b) is the 'soft box' or window effect, without the trans-illuminated background. The reflected highlight reveals the smooth inner surface of the bowl, but the outer surface detail remains obscure.

Lighting condition (c) replaces the 'soft box' with a single spotlight, equivalent to replacing the patch of sky through a window with a ray of sunlight. This lighting generates a distinctive shadow pattern, and refractions in the cut glass produce a lively highlight pattern. This scene emphasizes that the extent to which the lighting quality of 'sharpness' may be evident depends strongly on the attributes of the illuminated object.

Lighting condition (d) is due to multiple compact sources and takes us back to the jeweller's window. Multiple light refractions generate a complex highlight pattern, giving the glass bowl the

2.12a   2.12b

2.12c   2.12d

2.12e

Figure 2.12: *Effects of lighting upon the appearance of a cut crystal bowl. (a) The bowl stands on a trans-illuminated white plastic material which forms its background. (b) Flow of light from the right, due to a large diffusing light source with no back lighting. (c) Flow of light from right, due to a compact, directional light source. (d) Multiple compact sources. (e) Multiple compact sources with black background*

appearance of sparkle. Meanwhile the shadow pattern has lost its definition.

Lighting condition (e) is identical to (d), except for the change of background. The black background eliminates the shadow pattern, so that the bowl's appearance is due entirely to the highlight pattern that it generates.

The purpose of this study has been to examine effects due to changes in the directional distribution of lighting. We have discussed aspects of how the level of incident illumination may affect the appearance of displayed objects, and how the spectral distribution of illumination affects the perception of colours. It often happens in museum lighting that designers have little scope to modify either of these aspects of illumination. Their real scope for creativity lies in controlling the directional distribution of lighting, and the key to this is understanding the three lighting patterns and their relationship to revealing object attributes. The ability to recognize what are the critical visual attributes of a three-dimensional object, and to be able to visualize the distribution of lighting that will optimally reveal those attributes, is a key skill for a lighting designer. It may be noted that the examples used to examine the lighting patterns have all been monochrome, and it probably is true to say that good display lighting for three-dimensional objects would look good in black and white, even for coloured objects. Nor should we exclude from this approach those objects that we usually think of as being two-dimensional. The surfaces of most paintings, as well as all tapestries and collage works, interact with the spatial distribution of incident light, and due to this they interact with the perception of a viewer. For more discussion of the lighting patterns and how they influence object appearance, refer to Cuttle (2003).

Light-induced damage to objects 3

The control of degradation of museum objects due to light exposure fits within the broad field of risk assessment, and seen in this context, it is in competition for limited attention and funds. Risk assessment for museums has been reviewed by Jonathon Ashley-Smith, who found that 'Damage by light is easy to control' (1999, p. 226). While that might seem a reasonable assessment for a curator who is concerned to protect a collection from earthquakes, tsunami, atmospheric pollution and terrorist threats, the processes of light-induced degradation are far from simple, and if one accepts that a process to be controlled should first be understood, then we are faced with a complex situation.

There are two processes by which light-induced degradation occurs:

- photochemical reactions
- radiant heating effect.

Of these, the former is has the greater potential to cause damage.

Photochemical reactions

Photochemical reactions are chemical reactions which are initiated, assisted or accelerated by exposure to light. These reactions are permanent changes in the molecular structure of the irradiated object, for which the energy for the reaction is derived from the absorption of a photon. Photons have been discussed in the previous chapter, and it was noted that at shorter wavelengths, photon energy levels are higher. Different molecules have different photon energy thresholds, so that some materials are affected only by UV radiation, while other more responsive materials are affected by both UV and visible radiant energy.

The situation is made complicated by the many different types of chemical action that may be induced. There are circumstances in

Facing page: *Church of Santa Maria Novella, Florence*

which photolysis may occur, where the absorbed photon energy is sufficient to overcome the bonding force of a molecule and causes it to split. Generally this requires that wavelength is less than 300 nm, or that a biphotonic process occurs, in which two photons are received in such rapid succession that the effect is the sum of their energies. In any museum where both UV and illumination are controlled, photolysis is highly unlikely and may be disregarded. The ever-present problem is that absorbed photon energies will stimulate chemical reactions between the molecules that make up the object's substance, as such reactions are promoted by the presence of light, warmth, oxygen or moisture. The reactions may be chains of events which continue after the photons have been absorbed, as studies of degradation in dark conditions have shown that reactions are more prevalent during periods following exposure to light. We are disinclined to think of the environmental conditions that suit us as being causes of degradation, but the fact is that the ideal conditions for many of the materials that we seek to conserve in museums would not merely be uncomfortable for us, but would fail to support us.

It needs to be recognized that many museum objects have complex molecular structures, and this is particularly true for coloured materials. As was discussed in the previous chapter, colourants, which include pigments and dyes, are substances which have selective spectral absorption characteristics, and a highly selective characteristic requires molecules that are complex in structure, and as a consequence, potentially reactive. An oil painting, for example, comprises thousands of different types of molecules, and it is inevitable that exposing such objects to light will initiate, assist or accelerate chemical reactions. To monitor these reactions would be a horrendously complicated task, and so instead our knowledge of relationships between photochemical reactions and exposure is based on observation and measurement of physical changes.

The readily observed physical effects of light exposure are loss of colour and loss of strength. Usually it is loss of colour or fading that is noticed first, and for this reason most research has been based on measuring colour changes due to measured amounts of exposure. This is discussed in later sections of this chapter.

Radiant heating effect

Although the photon energy levels of infrared radiation are below the threshold levels for all but the most responsive materials likely to be displayed in museums, it is wrong to suppose that exposure has no effect. Some light sources, particularly those based on incandescence, which includes tungsten halogen lamps, emit more radiant power as IR than as visible light, and the absorbed energy causes surface temperature to rise. The main aim of maintaining constant air temperature and relative humidity in a museum is to keep materials dimensionally stable. Where there are diurnal or seasonal variations of temperature, materials with high coefficients of thermal expansion, such as plastics, undergo cyclic changes which cause stress where they connect to other materials. Variations in humidity can be even more damaging, as virtually all organic materials are hygroscopic so that migrations of water vapour occur when humidity changes. The results of dimensional changes are manifest in many ways, and include cracking, breaking down of glued joints in wooden objects, and separation of varnishes from substrates.

The effect of illuminating an object with an infrared-rich source, such as a halogen spotlight, is to locally raise the surface temperature, causing expansion and moisture migration. The surface returns to its original condition when that light is switched off, and repetition of this cycle every 24 hours is likely to accelerate degradation. The visible effects of this degradation are not easily distinguished from the effects of photochemical reactions, and so while it is generally acknowledged to be a much less pernicious source of damage, there is uncertainty over how much damage is caused by radiant heating effect. It may be expected that as museums become more rigorous in protecting their collections from UV, the effects of IR will become of more concern.

It can safely be assumed that the radiant heating effect of visible light at controlled illuminance levels in museums is not a significant source of damage. There are no handy meters for measuring IR levels, and really the most reliable way of assessing whether IR levels are sufficient to cause problems is by the time-honoured process of feeling the heating effect on the back of one's hand when held over the object. Ways of reducing IR levels are discussed in Chapter 7.

Material response to exposure

The scientific principles that relate light exposure to degradation of museum objects are stated in CIE Technical Report 157, *Control of Damage to Museum Objects by Optical Radiation* (CIE, 2004), and the next two sections are based on the content of that report.

As UV, visible light and IR are all forms of radiant power, their overall density of incidence on a surface is termed irradiance and may be quantified in watts per square metre, (W/m^2). The exposure of an object to radiant energy over a period of time is the product of irradiance and time, so that:

$$\text{Exposure (Wh/m}^2) = \text{Irradiance (W/m}^2) \times \text{Hours of exposure (h)}$$

This expression indicates the interchangeability of irradiance and time. It shows that if we halve the irradiance, it will take twice as long for the same level of exposure to occur.

To relate exposure to damage of an irradiated material, we need to take account of the material's response to incident radiant power, and it has been noted that wavelength is an important factor. Researchers in Berlin, Germany, have exposed a range of moderately responsive museum materials under controlled conditions, and have monitored resulting colour changes over time. From these they have derived a mathematical expression for the relative damage response of exposed materials according to wavelength of incident radiation, $D(\lambda)$, which shows that relative damage reduces by one logarithmic unit for every 200 nm increase in wavelength. This function is shown in Figure 3.1, where it can be seen that if $D(\lambda)$ is given an arbitrary value of one at 300 nm, then the value falls to 0.1 at 500 nm, and to 0.01 at 700 nm. The $D(\lambda)$ function can be compared with $V(\lambda)$, previously shown in Figure 2.1,

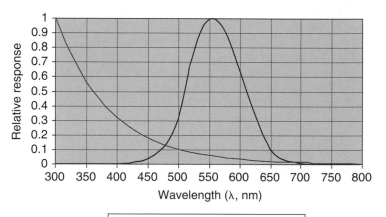

Figure 3.1: *The 'Berlin function' of relative damage potential according to wavelength, compared with relative visual response*

and it is apparent that the relative damage response of materials is very different from the human relative visual response. This means that illuminance is not a reliable indicator of exposure rate.

While the Berlin researchers concluded that this relative damage response curve describes the general trend well, they also found that the range of responses for more than 50 samples of museum materials was approximately one logarithmic unit, indicating that the most responsive materials in their study were approximately 10 times as responsive as the least responsive. The materials tested included rag paper, watercolours on rag paper, oil paints on canvas and textiles, of which the watercolours and textiles were most responsive and the rag paper the least.

While these data give us our best indication of the likely influence of wavelength on the response of an exposed material, this curve has to be treated with some caution. As all wavelengths shorter than 400 nm are UV, it appears to indicate that once UV has been eliminated there is little to worry about. This would be misleading. Certainly radiation at 300 nm has a high potential to cause damage, but even out of doors in full daylight the amount of radiant power at this wavelength is very low compared with the visible spectrum. Once we move indoors, ordinary window glass effectively eliminates wavelengths shorter that 315 nm, but it is common experience that furnishing fabrics exposed to sunlight are not protected from fading by window glass. The control of UV in the 315 to 400 nm range is discussed in Chapter 5.

Turning attention to the visible spectrum, it can be seen that short-wavelength power (blue light) is potentially more damaging than long-wavelength power (red light), and in the past this has encouraged museum staff to opt for incandescent lamps as the safe option. Lumen for lumen, incandescent lighting is a relatively safe option, but the low colour temperature may fail to provide satisfactory visual conditions. There are various reasons why this might be so. The lighting may fail to provide adequately for revealing the range of colours that occur in the object, or the lighting may appear unnatural to viewers who are adapted to daylight. These aspects are discussed further in Chapter 6.

The researchers have measured colour changes in exposed samples over time, and this is the basis of their measure of damage. It should be recognized that there is some danger in this. A material

Figure 3.2: *While this eighteenth century unfinished pastel portrait by Maurice-Quentin De La Tour shows no apparent evidence of exposure, the paper that supports it has been seriously affected (with permission of Musée Antoine Lécuyer, Saint-Quentin, France)*

that is structurally susceptible and which supports a light-fast colourant may show only slight effect of exposure while it is being physically weakened to a serious extent. An example of this is shown in Figure 3.2. This unfinished eighteenth century pastel portrait has been looked after carefully, as this type of artwork is notoriously fragile and yet its appearance is excellent. However, it was actually drawn onto blue paper, and the effect of exposure to daylight has not only totally faded the colour of the paper, but it has reduced the paper to a very brittle condition.

As it is the absorption of photons that stimulates the photo-chemical reactions, it follows that photons that are reflected at the surface have no damaging effect. As the curve shown in Figure 3.1 is an average of many responses, it is typical of neutral coloured materials which reflect light more or less uniformly at all wavelengths, and the decline in responsiveness at longer wavelengths is due to the decreasing photon energy levels. A red- or yellow-coloured material can be expected to show an even more pronounced decline at longer wavelengths as the surface reflects proportionally more photons at these wavelengths. Conversely, a blue-coloured material may be less responsive to short-wavelength visible light than to longer wavelengths, defying the trend shown in the figure. This underlines the problem of using typical or average response curves. Museum materials are diverse in their nature and their response characteristics, and in particular, colourants are materials chosen for their selective specular absorptance characteristics. While the Berlin curve gives an overall indication of the relative potential of light to cause damage to museum objects, there is no such thing as an average or typical material response. This curve may be used with caution for comparing the exposure due to alternative light sources, or for comparing the effectiveness of filters, but it should not be used for estimating the effect of exposing a particular material.

Limiting exposure

Several authorities (see Bibliography) have proposed broad categories of materials according to their responsiveness to exposure, and have applied these for the purpose of recommending limiting illuminance values. CIE 157:2004 defines four such categories, and the listing in Table 3.1 is based on this classification.

Whereas it might appear to be quite straightforward to apply Table 3.1 to classify actual museum objects, it is always advisable to consult a professional conservator. Assessment of responsiveness depends upon recognizing all the materials of which the object is composed and identifying the most light-responsive. Conservators may be guided by the ISO ratings of various materials, which are determined by the Blue Wool Test. This light-fastness test involves exposing material samples in a special light exposure cabinet alongside a standard card that holds eight dyed wool samples, and comparing the extent of fading at intervals. ISO 1 is the most responsive classification; ISO 2 is approximately half as responsive as 1SO 1; and so on to the ninth classification, which is for materials rated more than ISO 8. The ISO ratings can

Table 3.1 *Four category classification of materials according to responsiveness to visible light. (After CIE 157:2004)*

Material responsiveness classification	Material description
R0. Non-responsive	The object is composed entirely of materials that are **permanent**, in that they have no response to light. Examples: most metals, stone, most glass, genuine ceramic, enamel, most minerals
R1. Slightly responsive	The object includes durable materials that are **slightly light-responsive**. Examples: oil and tempera painting, fresco, undyed leather and wood, horn, bone, ivory, lacquer, some plastics
R2. Moderately responsive	The object includes fugitive materials that are **moderately light-responsive**. Examples: costumes, watercolours, pastels, tapestries, prints and drawings, manuscripts, miniatures, paintings in distemper media, wallpaper, gouache, dyed leather and most natural history objects, including botanical specimens, fur and feathers
R3. Highly responsive	The object includes **highly light-responsive** materials. Examples: silk, colorants known to be highly fugitive, newspaper

be related to the four responsiveness categories as indicated in Table 3.2.

The concept of a 'noticeable fade' upon which the data in Table 3.2 is based has been used extensively in light-fastness research. If samples of coloured materials are viewed side-by-side, it is the smallest colour difference for which the researchers would be able to expect reliable discrimination by a typical observer. For the technically minded, this step is defined as Grey Scale 4 (GS4), and is approximately equal to a colour difference of 1.6 CIELAB units. There are approximately thirty such steps in the transition from bright colour to white.

There are some useful insights to be gained from Table 3.2. Comparing the 'UV rich' and the 'No UV' data, it can be seen that

Table 3.2 *Years for noticeable fade for object on display 3000 hours per year at 50 lux. 'UV rich' refers to a spectrum similar to daylight through glass, and 'No UV' means no radiant power below 400 nm. See text for definitions of ISO ratings and a noticeable fade step. Based on data from CIE 157:2004*

Material responsiveness classification	ISO Rating	Years for noticeable fade	
		UV rich	No UV
R3. Highly responsive	1	1.5	2
	2	4	7
	3	10	20
R2. Moderately responsive	4	23	67
	5	53	200
	6	130	670
R1. Slightly responsive	7	330	2000
	8	800	7300

while it always is beneficial to filter out UV, the extent of added protection increases as responsiveness reduces. The reason for this is that the less responsive materials have higher photon energy thresholds, and so are less affected by visible light. This reinforces the message that UV control should be applied throughout museums, rather than being restricted to areas where moderately or highly responsive materials are displayed. The 'No UV' data applies only where all radiant power of wavelengths shorter than 400 nm is eliminated, and where there is uncertainty about this, the 'UV rich' data should be assumed to be appropriate. Materials rated as 'more than ISO 8' should not necessarily be classified as 'R0. Non-responsive'. Certainly their responsiveness is low, but their colour may not be permanent. There are few museum exhibits for which it is safe to assume that all materials, including the objects and their support materials, are totally non-responsive. It is generally prudent to eliminate UV and to control illumination, although as discussed in Chapter 4, exceptions may be made and can make very effective contributions to the overall experience of a museum visit.

All of these data are based on 3000 hours of display annually at an illuminance of 50 lux. Museums that expose their collections for less than 3000 h/y may increase the 'years for noticeable fade' values accordingly. As explained in Chapter 2, with care satisfactory viewing can be achieved with less than 50 lux, but this value

Table 3.3 *Limiting illuminance (lux) and limiting annual exposure (lux hours per year) for material responsiveness classifications*

Material responsiveness classification	Limiting illuminance (lx)	Limiting exposure (lx h/y)
R0. Non-responsive	no limit	no limit
R1. Slightly responsive	200	600 000
R2. Moderately responsive	50	150 000
R3. Highly responsive	50	15 000

is often used as a guide for providing acceptable colour discrimination with minimal light exposure. For the R2 category, this level of annual exposure results in reasonably slow rates of fading providing UV is eliminated, and this provides the base value for current illumination recommendations. As shown in Table 3.3, it may be expressed as a limiting illuminance of 50 lux or as a limiting exposure of $3000 \times 50 = 150\,000$ lux hours per year.

For the R3 classification, it is clear from Table 3.2 that even with UV elimination, fading rates at this level of exposure are excessive. It is not practical to overcome this by reducing illuminance, and so Table 3.3 specifies an annual limiting exposure value that is a mere 10 per cent of the R2 value. This can be achieved only by reducing the duration of exposure, which has the effect of increasing the 'years for noticeable fade' values tenfold.

For the R1 classification, the 'No UV' values in Table 3.2 appear very satisfactory, and here Table 3.3 permits some relaxation. As explained in Section 2.3, viewers prefer more than 50 lux and researchers have found that a significant increase in preference can be gained by increasing illuminance to 200 lux, beyond which preference continues to increase but at a reduced rate. Accordingly both the limiting illuminance and the limiting exposure are increased to permit this, and it should be noted that the effect will be to reduce the 'years for noticeable fade' values to one quarter of the levels shown in Table 3.2.

In this way, the relationships between the limiting levels in Table 3.3 and rates of fading differ according to the material responsiveness category, notwithstanding that in all cases other than R0 it is necessary for UV to be eliminated and illuminance to be restricted. For the R1 Slightly Responsive materials, the governing criterion is viewer preference; for R2 Moderately Responsive materials it is providing for adequate colour discrimination, and for R3 Highly Responsive materials it is avoidance of excessive exposure. The application of these limiting levels in museums is discussed in Chapter 9.

Daylighting typologies

4

The aesthetics of daylight

While there is an extensive body of literature dealing with everything from our physiological to our spiritual involvement with daylight, this chapter is concerned with ways in which designers admit daylight into museums to enable viewers to experience art, and what is different about that experience compared with using electric lighting.

Generally, a prime requirement is for the designer to eliminate direct sunlight being admitted to display spaces, as this is both visually distracting and a source of damaging exposure for most displayed objects. However, nobody should doubt the opportunities for display that are sacrificed by this decision. I took Figure 4.1 in the Atrium of the East Wing of the National Gallery, Washington, DC, and I can count myself as having been fortunate to be in that place at that time. While this is a public space rather than a gallery, it is used very effectively for displaying a few sculptures, and of course, they have to be composed entirely of materials that are non-responsive to light exposure. As bands of sunlight sweep through this space during the day, individual works can suddenly be brought to life by a fortuitous interaction of form and sunlight. The same sculptures displayed in the controlled illumination of a gallery space will never take on such an appearance.

Also we should not overlook the opportunities that a decision to admit daylight affords to architects. Who can fail to be struck by the beauty of Frank Lloyd Wright's skylight in the Guggenheim Museum, New York, shown in Figure 4.2? Nearby Marcel Breuer has opened up the interior of the Whitney Museum of Modern Art with distinctive trapezoidal windows (Figure 4.3). The apertures by which daylight is admitted may be developed as striking architectural elements, but again, this aspect of design is not discussed further in this chapter.

Facing page: *Portland Museum of Art, Portland, Maine*

Figure 4.1: *A group of sculptures in sunlight. National Gallery of Art, East Building, Washington, DC*

What designers are required to provide in daylit art galleries and museums is diffused daylight, stripped of its damaging UV content, and moderated to provide both comfortable viewing and an acceptably low rate of damage. While this may seem to be a severely limiting set of criteria, this chapter explains that in fact it provides considerable scope for differences of design philosophy. The generic diagrams of the principal typologies shown in Figure 4.4 may assist in following this chapter.

Figure 4.2: *Frank Lloyd Wright's skylight at the Guggenheim Museum, New York*

Figure 4.3: *Marcel Breuer's trapezoidal windows at the Whitney Museum, New York*

Figure 4.4: *Daylighting typologies: a thumbprint summary. The diagrams are not to scale*

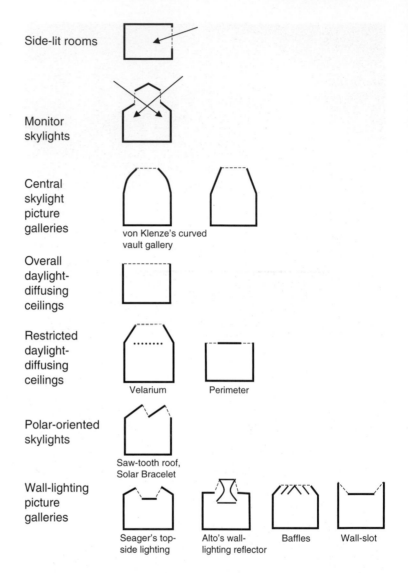

Side-lit rooms

Monitor skylights

Central skylight picture galleries

von Klenze's curved vault gallery

Overall daylight-diffusing ceilings

Restricted daylight-diffusing ceilings

Velarium   Perimeter

Polar-oriented skylights

Saw-tooth roof, Solar Bracelet

Wall-lighting picture galleries

Seager's top-side lighting   Alto's wall-lighting reflector   Baffles   Wall-slot

Side-lit rooms

The first art collections were gathered by medieval aristocrats, and among the greatest of these was the collection of the Medicis in the Pitti Palace, Florence. Under Lorenzo the Magnificent (1449–92), the collection developed to truly reflect the title ascribed to him. The wonderful thing is that the palace and its collection have survived intact. The Medicis were not vanquished nor did they fall into bankruptcy; instead their power was gradually subsumed by the state so that now the palace is state property and is open to the public with all its treasures intact.

Figure 4.5: *One of the decorated ceilings in the galleries of the Pitti Palace, Florence*

Once the doors open, a visitor who has taken the precaution of arriving well before opening time has the opportunity to spend a few minutes wandering through an amazing succession of rooms without being surrounded by other tourists. The rooms are connected one into the next in an enfilade down one side of the palace, then two rooms are linked across the end, and the progression continues back along the opposite side. In this way, all rooms except for the two end rooms are side-lit from windows in one wall. Fine mesh curtains are used to diffuse and moderate the incoming light, and although some electric lighting is used to

Figure 4.6: *The Hall of Mars at the Pitti Palace, showing a forward tilted painting on the facing wall*

highlight selected features, the flow of light from the windows is dominant. Not only does each room house a treasure trove of art, but it is itself a work of art. At first, one's eyes are drawn upwards by the magnificent painted ceilings (Figure 4.5), until attention is inevitably drawn down by the sumptuous works of art on the walls. In the Hall of Mars, Rubens' masterpiece *The Consequences of War* occupies prime position on the wall facing the windows (Figure 4.6) so that the flow of light from the windows draws attention to this favourably lit surface. However, the painting is not attached directly to the wall but is tilted forwards, and this can be seen quite clearly in the photograph. What is the reason for this?

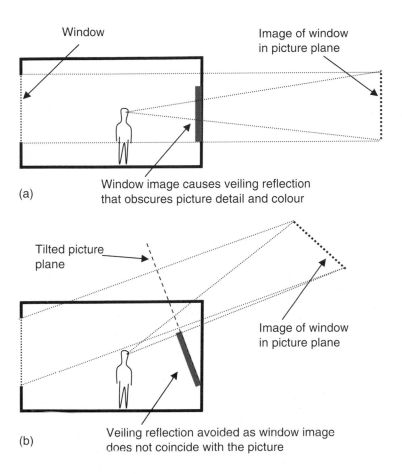

Window

Image of window
in picture plane

(a)

Window image causes veiling reflection
that obscures picture detail and colour

Tilted picture
plane

Image of window
in picture plane

(b)

Veiling reflection avoided as window image
does not coincide with the picture

Figure 4.7: *Veiling reflections in a side-lit room. (a) A picture facing the window fixed directly to the wall causes the image of the window to coincide with the picture. (b) The picture is tilted forward to avoid the veiling reflection*

Figure 4.7(a) shows a section through the room with the picture fixed directly to the wall. The picture may be treated as a plane mirror, for although the combined specular reflectance of the picture glass and the painted surface will be lower than that of a mirror, the same principles can be used to locate the virtual image of the window. The rule is that the image is as far behind the plane of the mirror as the object is in front of it, and from the viewer's position, this image will appear superimposed over the centre of the picture. The effect would be a veiling reflection that would obscure detail and drain the picture of colour. Figure 4.7(b) shows the effect of tilting the picture plane forward, and for this reflecting plane, the image would be located above the picture. This means that, in reality, no image of the window will be apparent. However, it should be noted that in this example, the critical dimensions that determine the tilt angle are the height of the picture, the height of the viewer, and the viewer's distance

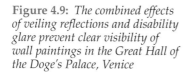

Figure 4.8: *A side tilted painting on a side wall, in the Hall of Mars*

from the picture, and in this case the tilt is only just sufficient. A shorter viewer, or a viewer who approaches closer, would see the reflected window image. Furthermore, it is not that no superimposed image will occur, but that it will be an image of the wall beneath the window and the floor, and reflective surfaces in this zone must be prevented if noticeable veiling reflections are to be avoided. The geometry of veiling reflections is examined in more detail in Chapter 7.

Returning to Figure 4.6, having satisfied ourselves that the appearance of the Rubens is free from distracting reflections, we shift our attention to works on the adjoining walls. Raphael's *The Lady of the Chair* catches our attention (Figure 4.8), and we note that this picture too is tilted, but this time it is hinged on one side so it can be tilted in the horizontal pane. The reason for tilting this picture is quite different. In the case of the Rubens, adequacy of illumination is not a problem as the picture faces directly towards the window, but for the Raphael light is incident at a glancing angle and particularly for pictures with deep frames, the light level on the picture surface may be well below the ambient level to which the viewer is adapted. To avoid a dull appearance, the picture is tilted towards the incident light, but if it is tilted too far, veiling reflections will become a problem. In this way we can see that it takes some manipulation to make side-lit rooms work even reasonably well for displaying pictures.

For further confirmation of this we can extend our trip to include the Doge's Palace, Venice. Vast scenes from the city's history of maritime victories and conquests are depicted on the walls of the Great Hall (Figure 4.9), but the viewing conditions are very poor. There are two reasons for this. The opposite side of the hall

Figure 4.9: *The combined effects of veiling reflections and disability glare prevent clear visibility of wall paintings in the Great Hall of the Doge's Palace, Venice*

comprises a continuous row of windows looking out over the Grand Canal and towards the Isle of San Magiore. Nobody would want to be denied this lovely view, and the windows give a strong flow of light within the space, but for the viewpoint in Figure 4.9 these windows provide massive veiling reflections. The other reason concerns the two apertures in the facing wall which open into a courtyard. They appear very bright, and because they occur immediately adjacent to the decorated wall surfaces, they cause disability glare (see Chapter 2), which is another veiling effect upon the appearance of the wall paintings. The combined effect of veiling reflections and disability glare is such that it is not possible to find a position that gives satisfactory viewing for this wall.

Figure 4.11: *Sculptures in a side-lit room at the Rodin Museum, Paris, France*

Even so, within this hall there is an example of excellent viewing. To experience it, we move to the centre of the hall and tilt our heads back to view the ceiling, and the scene in Figure 4.10 comes into view. The difference in appearance is startling, and is entirely due to the lighting. Here we have bi-directional lighting, with the dominant flow of light from the right (the direction of the window wall) but with sufficient light from the left to avoid excessively strong shadows, and a total lack of veiling reflections. As we gaze at the painting, the surface behind our heads is the floor, which is far too dark to cause a distracting veiling reflection. The result is a visually excellent, if physically uncomfortable, viewing situation.

This brings us to the first step in the evolution of the modern picture gallery. Instead of redirecting people's gaze upwards, the side-lit room has been rotated to create the skylit picture gallery, and the variety of ways in which designers have tackled skylighting occupies much of the remainder of this chapter. So dominant is the image of an art gallery comprising blank walls and overhead skylights that this is the instantly recognizable form of purpose-designed gallery buildings. Nonetheless, we should not lose sight

of the fact that side-lit rooms can work very well for sculpture. The Rodin Museum in Paris is housed in a converted mansion that has elegant windows looking out to the surrounding gardens (Figure 4.11), and the quality of the lighting provided onto Rodin's classic works is excellent. The shading patterns generated by the lateral flow of light reveal superbly the forms and textures of *The Kiss* (Figure 4.12) and give life to the dynamic forms of this famous sculpture. Overhead lighting would have been far less effective.

Figure 4.13: *Carlo Scarpa's side-lit hall for Canova's sculptures at the Gipsoteca Canoviana, Possagno, Italy, gives changing light and shade patterns as the sun makes its daily progression*

Of course the Rodin Museum was not designed for this purpose, but the Giposotecka Canovia is a rare example of a side-lit room specifically designed as a sculpture gallery. The museum directors had invited Carlo Scarpa to design a modest extension to their gallery, and he created the remarkable space shown in Figure 4.13. The sun's daily rotation around this gallery produces constantly changing patterns of light and shade on Canova's sculptures, giving an endless variety of interactions between direct sunlight, diffused skylight, inter-reflected light, and the sculptures.

Monitor skylights

The 1780 design for the Great Room of the Royal Academy in Somerset House, London, was based on monitor skylights that had become widely used in art sale rooms and in the private galleries that could be found in stately homes of the time. The aim was to achieve a crossover light distribution onto the walls, as indicated in Figure 4.4. Scharf's lively depiction of the 1828 exhibition, shown in Figure 4.14, shows the skylights clearly, and also the way in which every available patch of wall surface was employed for display. Pictures at eye level are mounted vertically, and those above are tilted forwards to reduce veiling reflections. To the left of the scene we can see how viewers coped with the situation. Some approached closely, even crouching to study paintings that are hung right down to skirting level, while others are shown standing well back to observe the paintings mounted high on the opposite wall. It is also clear that for some of the visitors, the attraction of the exhibition was that of a social occasion. Although the annual exhibition was held in summer, the hours of daylight were not sufficient for these visitors. In 1812 the Prince Regent had donated

Figure 4.14: *G. Scharf I,* The Royal Academy Exhibition, 1828 *(with permission, Museum of London)*

the massive candelabrum to the Royal Academy, with the aim of extending the duration of the viewing hours. At the time it had supported 30 oil lamps; it was converted to gas in 1817. Scharf's painting is a daytime scene, so that although the gas burners are in place they are not in use. The effect of this ball of fire upon viewing after dusk must have been devastating, not so much because of the changed distribution of illumination but because it would have been impossible to avoid both direct and reflected glare when viewing any pictures above eye level. Perhaps during the evenings, that was less important than the socializing, and we can only speculate whether the paintings or the visitors suffered more from the town gas combustion fumes.

It may be noted in passing that this type of picture hanging arrangement was not without contemporary critics. On 7 January 1847, John Ruskin proposed in a letter to *The Times* that all pictures should be glazed. His argument was that this would make it impossible to see pictures hung at high level due to veiling reflections from skylights, so that curators would be obliged to hang pictures in a single, or at the most double, line at eye level. He argued that not only would this improve the viewing conditions, but it would enable curators to arrange paintings in chronological order.

The Dulwich Art Gallery is sometimes said to be the first purpose-built picture gallery, and it came about by an unusual set of circumstances. Two London art dealers, Noel Desenfans and Francis Bourgeois, had been amassing a national art collection for the King of Poland, Stanislas Augustus, until the partition of Poland in 1795 left the dealers unpaid and with a substantial number of paintings. Rather than selling the collection, Bourgeois added more paintings before he bequeathed it in 1811 to Dulwich College, a private school in south London, with a few provisos. A gallery was to be constructed to house not only the collection, but also the tombs of the gallery founders, being himself, his colleague Desenfans, and his wife. Thus the architect was confronted with designing a public picture gallery, for which there was no precedent, combined with a mausoleum, for which of course there were many precedents.

The choice of Sir John Soane for architect was fortunate indeed. Soane was fascinated with the manifold ways of admitting daylight into buildings, and his own home, now the Sir John Soane Museum and open to the public, stands as a testimony to his inventiveness. In a narrow building of a terraced row of houses on a London square, he had incorporated lantern skylights, domes,

Figure 4.15: *The Dulwich Picture Gallery, 1849*

'floating' ceilings that admit light around their perimeters, and glazed panels to transfer light between spaces, sometimes washing surfaces with coloured light. To this day, it is an inspirational visit for anyone interested in daylighting.

The Dulwich Picture Gallery opened its doors in 1814, and a print from 1849 (Figure 4.15) probably is fairly close to the original appearance. Three identifying features of Soane's design are visible:

- rectangular-plan galleries connected by archways on a central axis, providing views through several gallery spaces

- the cornice top of each picture hanging wall is connected to a central skylight by a sloping ceiling vault with deep indentations

- a monitor skylight with glazed vertical surfaces and an opaque top.

Soane was following tradition with his skylight design, with the aim of producing a 'crossover' daylight distribution that would direct incoming light on to the wall surfaces. However, contemporary reports indicate that visitors complained about the lack of light. Richard Redgrave, Surveyor of the Queen's pictures, made proposals in 1858 to improve conditions in the gallery, which included filling in the indentations in the ceiling vault to make it continuous; introducing a 'varied' colour scheme; and adding glazing to the upper sloping sections of the skylight. The latter recommendation was acted upon 'in the Edwardian era', with glazing being added to the upper sloping section of the skylight. The gallery was extensively damaged by bombing in the Second World War, and when it was rebuilt, the skylight was restored not to its original form, but to its modified form with glazing in both its vertical and sloping surfaces.

Figure 4.16 shows the present appearance of one of the gallery spaces, and because it is not possible to show clearly both the interior and the skylight in the same photograph, the skylight is shown in Figure 4.17. The indentations in the ceiling vault are still there, and while the décor has undergone several changes over the years to suit changing fashions, the current scheme is believed to closely resemble Soane's original design for the interior. The opening up of part of the top section of the lantern skylight not only increased the admission of daylight into the gallery, but also changed the daylight distribution. Light onto the walls would be increased, but by a lesser proportion than light onto the floor. The overall effect of this change would be more towards the impression of a well-lit space, than towards the appearance of well-lit pictures. That seems to be what was wanted. The skylight has been rebuilt again since the immediate post-war period, this time to meet security requirements, but there seems no enthusiasm for changing back to Soane's original concept.

Figure 4.16: *One of Soane's daylit galleries at the Dulwich Picture Gallery, London, UK*

Figure 4.17: *The skylight at the Dulwich Picture Gallery was originally a monitor skylight, and has been modified with glazing in the sloping roof elements*

The problem with the monitor skylight is that the crossover day-light distribution simply does not work. To avoid direct sunlight on to the pictures, the glazing has to be diffusing or fitted with diffusing blinds. That means that the source of illumination for a picture mounted on the wall, instead of being a patch of sky visible through a clear glazed skylight, becomes a pane of diffusing glass that spreads its light uniformly. The result is a suffusion of diffused light in the region of the skylight, and declining light levels towards the lower regions of the walls where the pictures hang.

Although the Dulwich Gallery is not on the main tourist itineraries, it is a favourite with Londoners. It evokes warm comments relating to its sense of intimacy and human scale, and this certainly would distinguish it from the major art institutions of the city. Rather amusingly, it would appear that this characteristic was not admired, or even wanted, in the nineteenth century. Just a glance back to compare Figure 4.14 with Figure 4.16 will confirm that the artist had miniaturized the occupants, thereby creating an impression of grandeur that was quite false.

Central skylight picture galleries

While central skylights come in a variety of forms, the problem with them is all about proportions. If the ratio of height to width is too low, veiling reflections become apparent in the upper parts of the pictures. If the ratio is made higher, then the best-lit surfaces in the gallery are the upper walls and the floor, and the poorest-lit surfaces are the lower walls where the pictures hang.

When Otto von Klenze was considering his options for the original Pinakotek museum to be built in Munich, he would have been aware of Soane's gallery, but the differences of scale called for much rethinking. Not only was the Pinakotek to be an altogether larger institution, but there was a need to accommodate much larger art works. This question of scale is an important factor in the design of galleries. Large paintings need a large space to give a sense of them being properly accommodated, and this raises practical viewing issues. Viewers need to be able to stand further back to visually take in the extent of the picture, so that galleries have to be wider, but also while large paintings extend not much further below the viewer's eye level, they extend much further above, and in top-lit galleries, this spells trouble with veiling reflections. It is the occurrence of reflections in upper parts of the pictures that is the problem, and Figure 4.18 compares the gallery proportions that are necessary to avoid this occurrence in tall pictures for overall and central skylights.

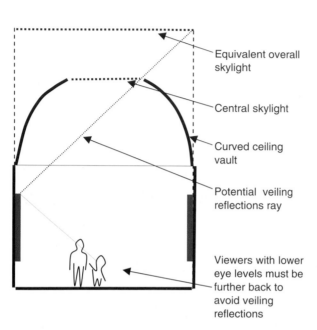

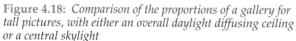

Equivalent overall
skylight

Central skylight

Curved ceiling
vault

Potential veiling
reflections ray

Viewers with lower
eye levels must be
further back to
avoid veiling
reflections

Figure 4.18: *Comparison of the proportions of a gallery for tall pictures, with either an overall daylight diffusing ceiling or a central skylight*

Figure 4.19: *The enfilade of gallery spaces at the Alte Pinakotek, Munich*

* A laylight is a secondary skylight. A skylight set into a roof may admit daylight directly into an interior space, or into a roof space which is connected to an interior space by a laylight.

von Klenze devised a grand succession of galleries giving long axial views (Figure 4.19). The rectangular floor plans were near-square; the hanging walls tall; and rising above these are smooth, curved ceiling vaults ascending to the skylight (Figures 4.20, 4.21). For the skylight itself, he opted for a flat, diffusing laylight*. By making the spaces tall and opting for near-square plans, he ensured that the skylights would be above the veiling reflection zone for viewing all four walls. A problem with diffusing skylights used in this way is that adjacent surfaces of the upper vault and the facing surface of the floor would be relatively strongly illuminated, and the weakest illumination would be on the hanging wall. von Klenze's solution for the vault is ingenious. Figure 4.22 compares a flat and a curved vault. For the flat vault, the illuminance will be greatest at point A and will decline through B to the least illuminated point at C. For the curved vault, the surface at point D is closest to the laylight, but it is tilted away from the incident light, and while F is furthest away, it is inclined toward the light. According to the proportions of the laylight and its diffusing characteristics, a curve can be devised that would give uniform illuminance from D through E to F. It is not being suggested that von Klenze actually predicted the contour by calculation, but it can be reasonably assumed that he understood the principle of what he was doing. Perhaps he conducted a few experiments to find a curve that produced the effect he wanted.

Figure 4.20: *von Klenze's central skylight with deep, curved ceiling vault at the Alte Pinakotek*

Figure 4.21: *The tall picture hanging space at the Alte Pinakotek*

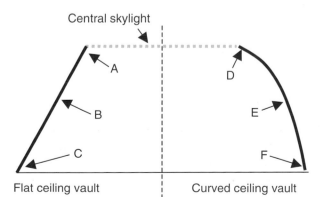

Figure 4.22: *Comparison of flat and curved ceiling vaults (see text for explanation)*

The overall effect for a visitor to von Klenze's gallery is a succession of tall, lofty galleries and hanging walls washed with overhead light. Veiling reflections due to the laylight are generally avoided unless one approaches close to a tall painting and looks upwards, and while the laylight is undeniably bright, the geometry of the space makes it unobtrusive (and very difficult to photograph). The most likely source of troublesome reflections is one's own light-coloured clothing, and that of other visitors. The floors are well-lit, and generally this promotes a sense of lightness and spaciousness, which is pleasant. This gallery too was damaged by Second World War bombing, and it has been faithfully restored to its original form.

Figure 4.23: *Galleries at the Kunsthistorisches Museum, Vienna, differ in architectural style from von Klenze's galleries, but conform closely in design principles*

von Klenze's gallery has been very influential and the form of its deep, curved vault has been reproduced many times around the world. At the Kunsthistorisches Museum, von Klenze's unadorned architecture has been replaced by baroque splendour, but the geometry remains faithful to von Klenze's concept (Figure 4.23). The importance of the geometry is illustrated at the Huntington Gallery (1910, architect Myron Hunt). The large gallery space shown in Figure 4.24 is devoted to British art, and half way down the wall to the right of this view hangs Thomas Gainsborough's *Blue Boy* (Figure 4.25). A dark painting such as this is very susceptible to veiling reflections, but in this instance they are quite

Figure 4.24: *The central skylight and curved ceiling vault at the main gallery at the Huntington Gallery, Pasadena, California*

Figure 4.25: *Gainsborough's* Blue Boy *hangs on a side wall at the Huntington Gallery, and is free from veiling reflections*

Figure 4.26: *Reynold's* Mrs Siddons as the Tragic Muse *hangs on an end wall, and visibility is affected by veiling reflections*

unobtrusive. The appearance of the picture is somewhat darkened by the light-coloured wall that forms its visual surround, but this apart, the viewing conditions are good. Pride of place on the end wall of the gallery, visible in Figure 4.24 and shown in detail in Figure 4.26, is Sir Joshua Reynolds' *Mrs Siddons as the Tragic Muse*. In this case the effect of veiling reflections is clearly evident and detracts significantly from the appearance of the painting. The difference is that in this case the viewing direction is along the long axis of the room, so that the reflected image of the bright laylight is much more extensive and intrudes over much of the picture. von Klenze avoided this effect by his use of tall, lofty rooms and division of the space into a succession of near-square floor plans.

Until the second half of the twentieth century, the technology employed in these galleries was simple. When the American philanthropist, Andrew Mellon, was considering the gallery that he would donate to his nation, he sent his architect John Russell Pope across to Europe to see what was best in gallery design, and Pope came back with von Klenze's concept in mind. The gallery, now the West Building of the National Gallery on the Constitution Mall, opened its doors in 1940. Figure 4.27 shows a typical gallery, in this instance the art works are not of the monumental size that von Klenze had to accommodate so the space has been scaled down to provide comfortable viewing, and generally veiling reflections are avoided. This effect has been achieved by simple means. Figure 4.28 shows the roof space above, where the skylight is reminiscent of an industrial greenhouse. This large expanse of glass is totally concealed from view at street level, where the building presents windowless facades, but at this level the glazing extends right across the building and for much of the time provides an abundance of daylight onto the laylights below. On the occasion of this visit, the skies were heavily overcast and the electric lighting was in use. These are the original 1940 incandescent floodlights, and although they have since been replaced by fluorescent luminaires, the means for controlling this installation remain simple.

Figure 4.27: *A central skylight with curved vault at the National Gallery of Art, West Building, Washington, DC*

When James Stirling was commissioned to design the Neue Staatsgalerie (1984), Stuttgart, to form an extension to the Alte Staatsgalerie, the director insisted that the interiors of the new galleries were to be similar to the gallery spaces in the existing gallery, which had been designed in accord with von Klenze's principles. Stirling took account of this instruction, and he worked with the team of German engineers that had been allocated to the project, and who ensured that technology would be to the fore in devising the means for environmental control.

The roof glazing is arranged in long runs of shallow-pitched skylights oriented on the north–south axis (Figure 4.29), the skylights being assemblies of sealed double-gazed panels. Each panel comprises:

- an upper pane of clear glass
- an air gap containing a sheet of glass fibre material to diffuse the light
- a lower pane of UV absorbing glass.

The light transmission factor for these panels is 20 per cent.

In the roof space beneath the skylights is a layer of motorized louvres (Figure 4.30). All the louvre blades are aligned on the north–south axis, and the light to each gallery is controlled by two photocells mounted on opposite gallery walls. These are set to maintain 200 lux incident on the walls, and motorized controls operate the louvres over each gallery in two halves, one to the

Figure 4.29: *Roof glazing at the Staatsgaleries, Stuttgart*

Figure 4.30: *Underside of the roof glazing and upper surface of the motorized light control louvres at the Staatsgaleries*

Figure 4.31: *Underside of the louvres and upper surfaces of the gallery laylights at the Staatsgaleries*

east and one to the west. This photo was taken before noon, looking north, so the louvres are inclined to intercept sunlight from the east. At around midday, the louvres will roll over to reverse the slope and intercept sunlight from the west.

At the next level down, we see the underside of the louvres and the topsides of the laylights (Figure 4.31). This space is air-conditioned to restrict peak summer temperatures to 25–27°C and minimum winter temperatures to 15–17°C, and this is part of a strategy for maintaining year-round temperatures in the gallery spaces of 21°C ± 3°. The laylights are triple-glazed, comprising:

- upper pane of clear glass
- air gap containing sheet of UV absorbing plastic
- pane of light diffusing glass
- air gap
- pane of laminated safety glass.

Figure 4.32: *A gallery space at the Staatsgaleries*

Finally we descend to the gallery level (Figure 4.32). Stirling may have matched some aspects of the appearance of the Alte Staatsgalerie, but we can see at a glance that von Klenze's concept has not survived. The curved ceiling vault has been reduced to a frieze, and as such has become one of the architect's vocabulary of eclectic symbols that is one of the characteristics of his architecture, as can be seen in the archway in this view. The proportions of this space do not accord with von Klenze's principles for avoiding veiling reflections.

More recently, some architects have returned to the concept of the central skylight with a view to recreating the distributions of light achieved by Soane and von Klenze, but it should not be overlooked that they have the comfortable advantage of knowing that electric lighting will be available to supplement the picture illumination on dull days, and even to give some subtle emphasis to selected works on brighter days, if this is required.

For the Sainsbury Wing at the National Gallery, London, where photography is not permitted, Robert Venturi opted for central lantern skylights. Whether he intended a link to Soane's gallery in south London is not known, but it seems that he had envisaged 'handsome, lofty lanterns that allow glimpses of sky'. However, the need to control and diffuse daylight led to the lanterns actually being constructed within a glazed 'attic', which enabled light to each of the lanterns to be controlled by motorized louvres, and the lanterns themselves were fitted with diffusing glass to conceal these devices. The ceiling vault, between the wall cornice and the lantern, is straight-sided, and has a light grey finish that appears to be a noticeable step darker than the hanging wall.

Figure 4.33: *A gallery space with central skylight and deep, flat ceiling vault at the Getty Center, Santa Monica, California*

For the Getty Center (1997), Richard Meier created tall, lofty spaces with central skylights that appear to have much in common with von Klenze's concept (Figure 4.33). The very deep ceiling vault has no curve, and is painted white to soften the contrast to the skylight, and this form is a strong architectural feature of these galleries. The skylights are clear-glazed and give a view through to the brilliant Californian sky. A single layer of motorized louvres beneath the glazing works very well. During several visits to the Getty Center, I have always found these louvres to be effectively blocking direct sunlight and maintaining an illuminance of 200 lux

Figure 4.34: *A deep, curved ceiling vault flows seamlessly from the walls to the central lantern skylight at the Samslung Essel, Klosterneuberg, Austria*

around the mid-points of the hanging walls. The geometry of these galleries ensures that the skylights are not sources of disability glare or veiling reflections, but reflections of the white vault can cause distracting reflections, notably in tall, dark-coloured paintings.

For the Samslung Essel, architect Heinz Tesar eliminated the cornice so that von Klenze's curved ceiling vault flows seamlessly from the walls, to be surmounted by a tall, lantern skylight (Figure 4.34). The walls and vault are rendered in flat white, and the pattern softly reveals the flow of light from the skylight and delineates the hanging wall. The skylight itself is clear glazed, but all of the glazing is obscured by fabric roller blinds. Fluorescent lighting has been neatly incorporated adjacent to the lower edge of the glazing, keeping the lanterns free from spotlights.

Central skylights remain the dominant form of daylighting for picture galleries, despite the difficulties in providing an illumination distribution that fully supports the process of viewing the pictures.

Overall daylight-diffusing ceilings

The wish to have daylight illumination, coupled with the need to eliminate direct sunlight, might suggest that the overall, daylight-diffusing skylight would be an obvious solution. However, examples are not very plentiful, and in some instances overall ceilings have been ripped out and replaced with more restricted areas of skylight.

The Oxford Natural History Museum is an exuberant example of nineteenth century Victorian Gothic architecture realized in the then-new media of steel and glass (Figure 4.35). To walk among the fossilized remains of these extinct giants in this cathedral-like setting suffused with light is a memorable experience, but of

Figure 4.35: *Victorian gothic architecture provides overall daylight diffusion at the Natural History Museum, Oxford*

Figure 4.36: *The Sculpture Court with daylight diffusing roof at the Louvre, Paris*

course there are no opportunities for displaying even slightly light-responsive exhibits in this setting. Shading, or other means of reducing illumination to a level that would satisfy conservators, would create severe visual adaptation problems.

A similar level of freedom pertains for displays of sculpture, and the great Sculpture Court at the Louvre offers a similar spatial experience while providing very satisfactory viewing conditions for the artworks (Figure 4.36). In spaces such as this, the selection of surface reflectances effectively determines the strength of the shading patterns that will be generated by the sculptures. The flow of light is predominantly vertically downwards, although somewhat inclined towards the walls at the perimeter. The strength of shading patterns depends on how much of the downward light is reflected back upwards. A dark floor will give strong shading patterns, and a light floor will give soft, diffused lighting effects which can produce beautiful interactions with smoothly contoured

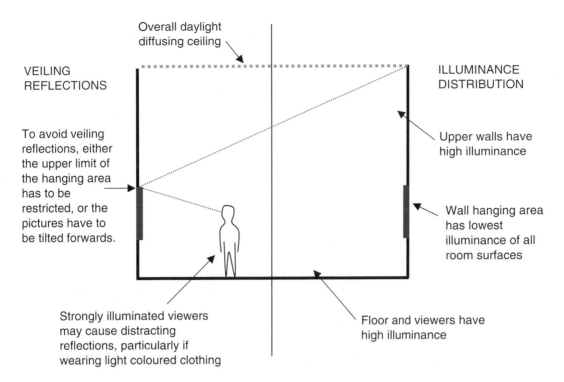

VEILING
REFLECTIONS

Overall daylight
diffusing ceiling

ILLUMINANCE
DISTRIBUTION

To avoid veiling
reflections, either
the upper limit of
the hanging area
has to be
restricted, or the
pictures have to
be tilted forwards.

Upper walls have
high illuminance

Wall hanging area
has lowest
illuminance of all
room surfaces

Strongly illuminated viewers
may cause distracting
reflections, particularly if
wearing light coloured clothing

Floor and viewers have
high illuminance

sculptures, but there will be a lack of sharpness. Differences between glossy and matt surfaces, if evident at all, will be softly revealed, and some judicious use of spotlight luminaires may be beneficial.

The limitations associated with overall daylight-diffusing sky-lights become much more evident when they are applied for lighting two-dimensional artworks. The situation is summarized in Figure 4.37, and the good sense that underlies central skylight systems is evident. Nonetheless, the overall appearance of light-ness that can be engendered by overall skylights continues to attract architects.

Stirling and Francine Clark were a husband and wife team who started collecting art in the 1920s, and who commissioned a white marble art gallery in their home town of Williamstown, Massachusetts, which they subsequently bequeathed, with their collection, to their nation. Figure 4.38 gives a general view of one of the main exhibition rooms at the Clark Institute, showing the overall daylight-diffusing ceiling, which actually extends to form a curved ceiling vault running down to the cornice, and this extensive expanse of luminous material is clearly seen to be sup-plemented by electric lighting. The effect of the lighting in giving visual emphasis to the pictures is evident, and the close-up view

Figure 4.37: Potential veiling reflection and illuminance distribution problems for overall daylight diffusing ceilings in picture galleries

Figure 4.38: *The overall daylight diffusing ceiling at the Stirling and Francine Clark Institute, Williamstown, Massachusetts, merges into the upper walls*

Figure 4.39: *Supplementary electric lighting to give 'sharpness' to the diffused daylighting at the Clark Institute*

of the sculpture, Edgar Degas' *Little Dancer aged Fourteen* (Figure 4.39), shows the effect of the spotlights in generating sharply defined highlights on the dark, polished surface of the bronze casting. Without this, the appearance of the bronze would be lacking both form and texture. In acknowledging this need to supplement diffused daylight with electric lighting for every artwork on display, we start to gain some clues as to what is required for a satisfactory viewing experience in situations where there is ample, diffused daylight. This is a complex and subtle issue, and will be returned to in Chapter 6.

Not all installations of overall skylights have been as successful. Overall luminous ceilings became fashionable in commercial buildings during the 1960s and 1970s, and this might have encouraged some art institutions to install overall daylight-diffusing skylights as if they were the ultimate answer to museum lighting. The Metropolitan Museum of Art, New York, installed a large overall ceiling in the André Meyer Gallery displaying nineteenth century European paintings. The ceiling comprised 600 mm square clear prismatic plastic panels mounted some 2–3 m below a diffusing glass roof and approximately 6 m above floor level. Figure 4.40 shows the space on a bright day, when there is clearly an overall sufficiency of light. It can be seen that the space was subdivided by approximately 4 m high display panels. As the daylight faded, incandescent spotlights providing selective illumination onto the artworks automatically switched on (Figure 4.41). Although the museum had heralded this installation with something of a fanfare, it never really caught on with the viewing public. Some criticized

Figure 4.40: *During bright weather, this ceiling at the André Meyer Gallery in the Metropolitan Museum of Art, New York, used to provide overall diffused daylight*

Figure 4.41: *When daylight faded, automatic controls added localized electric lighting at the André Meyer Gallery*

the total lack of intimacy in the viewing conditions, and others the abrupt change-over between the two forms of lighting. Not long after I took these photographs in 1987, the entire space was reconstructed as a series of smaller galleries with central skylights.

As already mentioned, the potential of overall daylight-diffusing skylights to give an overall sense of lightness continues to attract designers. This was undoubtedly achieved on a restricted site at the Deutches Architecture museum (Figure 4.42), but to see how this impression might be achieved in a large space we turn to the Lentos Museum. This museum was the outcome of an architectural design competition, and the winning design placed all the display spaces on a single floor, elevated above the flood level of the adjacent River Danube, and with overall daylight-diffusing skylights throughout.

Figure 4.43 shows the rooftop of the building, with the River Danube in the background. Lines of near-horizontal glazing, 1.1 m wide and at 2.7 m centres, extend the full length of the building to give a total 940 linear metres of skylight, equivalent to approximately 30 per cent of the total gallery floor area. Figure 4.44 shows the skylight, which comprises:

- 8 mm clear glass top pane

- 29 mm air gap housing motorized louvres

Figure 4.42: *The overall daylight diffusing ceiling at the Deutches Architecture Museum, Frankfurt, approaches a hemispherical sky*

Figure 4.43: *Roof glazing at the Lentos Museum, Linz, Austria. The museum stands on the edge of the River Danube*

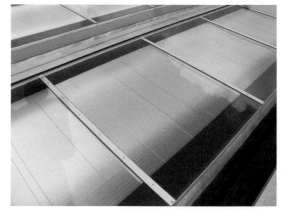

Figure 4.44: *Motorized light control louvres are incorporated into a hermetically sealed air gap in the roof glazing at the Lentos Museum*

- 6 mm clear glass
- 16 mm gap filled with argon gas
- 6 mm clear glass
- 0.76 mm UV-absorbing plastic film
- 6 mm sand-blasted glass.

Figure 4.45 shows the plenum space, with the skylights above and the translucent ceiling below. The resident engineer, Rainer Schrammel, is inspecting the electric lighting installation, and it may be noted that he dons white cotton overshoes before stepping onto the ceiling. The laminated glass ceiling panels comprise:

- 8 mm sand-blasted glass top pane
- 1.52 mm UV-absorbing plastic film
- 10 mm clear glass
- 1.52 mm UV-absorbing plastic film
- 10 mm clear glass.

Figure 4.45: *The underside of the roof glazing and the upper surface of the daylight diffusing ceiling at the Lentos Museum*

Figure 4.46 shows the largest of the gallery spaces below. At the time of my visit, there was a display of photographs of summer beach scenes that had been printed onto large panels of acrylic plastic. The overall sense of lightness was conducive to enjoyment of these images, and generally, the presentation was very successful. The ambient illuminance was 900 lux, and I discussed this with the resident engineer. He explained that they had in the past tried turning down the light level to meet a conservator's demands, but they found that an illuminance of less than 300 lux made the gallery appear unacceptably gloomy. Generally they set the controls to maintain the illuminance between 800 and 1000 lux, and it is clear that active control is needed to maintain day time illuminance values within this range. He also informed me that, on a clear sunny day, he had recorded 78 000 lux incident on the top surface of the skylights, and that this external condition with the louvres fully open gave 8000 lux in the large gallery.

The Lentos Museum clarifies the real issue with overall daylight-diffusing skylights. The viewer adapts to the brightness of the ambient field of view. The overall ceiling is brightest; usually the upper walls will be next; and after that the floor and the artworks hanging on the walls. If the ambient illuminance is high enough to give a satisfying sense of overall lightness, then all may be well. But if not, the space will appear gloomy and the appearance of

Figure 4.46: *A gallery space at the Lentos Museum. At the time this photograph was taken, the illuminance was 900 lux*

the artworks will be dull. If the ambient illuminance is set to satisfy conservation criteria, failure is inevitable.

So what is the point of constructing galleries of this type? First it needs to be noted that the Lentos Museum has gone to considerable lengths to ensure that the daylight in the galleries is free from UV, so that paintings displayed in the galleries would suffer significantly less exposure than if displayed in a matching level of outdoor daylight. Next, consider artworks in the R1 Slightly Responsive range (Table 3.1, p.46) for which the limiting exposure is 600 000 lx h/y. For an illuminance of 1000 lux, the limit is 600 hours of exposure per year, and for a gallery that is open 10 hours per day, that is two months per year. Or alternatively, two years per decade. So if an exhibition of low responsivity artworks really would look very good at 1000 lux, then why not? Providing, of course, the artworks are kept in light-proof storage for the rest of the time.

Finally, there is another question that goes beyond the scope of this book, but it will be raised anyway. Do we have to presume that every artwork that is displayed in a museum must be conserved? In the times when photography was based on film, the photographer's artwork was a signed exhibition-quality print, and any museum should treat it as an item to be conserved. While the photographer would be expected to archive the negative, it represented only a step on the way to producing the finished work. Consider the prints on display at the Lentos Museum. The photographer's images are stored as data files, and may be used to produce printed or projected images in a variety of media. Do the images on display need to be preserved for posterity once they have fulfilled the needs of the current display? I do not proffer an answer to this question, but I suggest that our range of visual experiences of art is enriched by opportunities to see some presentations mounted in spaces that have a suffusion of light.

To summarize the characteristics of overall daylight-diffusing skylights for picture galleries, visitors entering the space adapt to the brightness of the ceiling and upper walls, and also to that of the floor unless it is dark in colour. Pictures have to be restricted to the lower parts of the walls to avoid unacceptable veiling reflections, and so are noticeably in the poorest lit zones of the gallery. If the light level is raised to achieve an overall satisfactory sense of brightness, the illuminance on the pictures is likely to be far in excess of recommended levels. Lowering the light level to comply with conservation limits is likely to produce an overall appearance that would be judged dull or even gloomy.

Notwithstanding, there are situations, such as the Lentos Museum, where this need for high lighting levels is not merely tolerated, but is promoted for the sheer pleasure that is to be derived from experiencing art in an abundance of daylight. In other situations, the characteristics of overall daylight-diffusing skylights will be seen as shortcomings, and here the key to overcoming them is to restrict the amount of light entering the space, and to direct the light onto the artworks and other selected features. The objective is to lower the viewer's state of visual adaptation so that objects lit to restricted illuminance levels appear acceptably bright. While this is easily achieved by electric lighting, daylighting solutions are inevitably more elaborate, and designers need to appreciate that if control of daylit is carried to excess, viewers may fail to recognize that they are in a daylit space.

Restricted daylight-diffusing ceilings

There are various ways in which designers have employed restricted areas of daylight-diffusing ceiling, or have modified the distribution of light from overall ceilings. In the late nineteenth and early twentieth centuries, a simple expedient was to add a velarium, comprising a sheet of diaphanous fabric draped across the space beneath the skylight. The purpose was to both diffuse and redistribute the incoming daylight. A more sophisticated version of the velarium was installed at the Rijksmuseum, Amsterdam, for Rembrandt's masterpiece, *The Night Watch*, and is shown in Figure 4.47. The space has a central skylight below which a grey

Figure 4.47: *The light distribution of a central skylight has been modified by a velarium at the Rijksmuseum, Amsterdam (with permission, Rijksmuseum)*

glass velarium attenuates light onto the central floor area and any viewers, while light around the perimeter of the velarium washes down the walls. Although this photograph shows the arrangement of the velarium clearly, the effect of the photographer's photo-floods on the light distribution is evident. The Rijksmuseum has recently been closed for a major renovation, so the velarium may be gone when the gallery reopens.

For its North Wing extension, the National Gallery, London, divided the space into a series of fairly small galleries, each with a perimeter daylight-diffusing ceiling. Figure 4.48 shows that

Figure 4.48: *A perimeter skylight in the North Wing of the National Gallery, London. The dropped central ceiling has electric lighting incorporated around its edge*

Figure 4.49: *Above the perimeter skylight in the North Wing, two levels of motorized louvres arranged at right angles to each other control daylight illuminance in the gallery below*

Figure 4.50: *A small gallery area to one side of a circulation route with skylight above, at the Getty Center, Santa Monica, California*

Figure 4.51: *The central zone of this gallery space is lit by daylight, and the peripheral zone by electric lighting, at the Simon Norton Museum, Pasadena, California*

Figure 4.52: *Another example of a restricted area of skylight giving two distinct lighting zones at the Simon Norton Museum*

this arrangement effectively reduces downward light to the central floor area, but also it can be seen that there is a significant gradation of illumination down the walls, and that the pictures mounted above eye level have been noticeably tilted to avoid veiling reflections. The engineering of this installation (Figure 4.49) involves two layers of motorized louvres at right angles to each other beneath the skylight and a controlling photocell is visible on one of the supporting struts. The recessed area between the rows of laylights corresponds to the central ceiling in the galleries, and fluorescent lighting is installed around its perimeter. The control system enables a set wall illuminance in the gallery of 50 lux to be maintained within the limits of ±5 lux during normal daylight hours, and with the level being automatically supplemented by the fluorescent lighting when daylight fades.

There are examples of galleries making use of restricted areas of skylights to achieve quite different effects. One recurring use is to daylight an area that is to one side of a thoroughfare, and by raising the skylight above sightlines, impact may be given to a selected group of objects. The small group of sculptures at the Getty Center shown in Figure 4.50 occurs at a transition point between two larger display areas.

At the Simon Norton Museum, restricted areas of skylight are used to divide the space into distinct viewing zones (Figures 4.51, 4.52). At the centre, the skylight provides a cone of light onto sculpture displays and seating for weary viewers, while around the perimeter of the galleries electric lighting provides controlled illumination onto the paintings.

Polar-oriented skylights

Daylight-diffusing skylights receive the sum of direct sunlight, blue-sky light and cloud-reflected light, all of which is diffused by translucent materials. Polar-oriented skylights use orientation and external shading elements to prevent direct sunlight reaching the glazing, so that the source of light is diffused daylight from the sky. This has several advantages. The source of light is much less variable throughout the day than when direct sunlight is included. Because solar heat gains are minimal, larger glazing areas can be used without incurring summer overheating problems, and this enables satisfactory daylight levels to be maintained for greater proportions of normal daylight hours, even during overcast weather. Because the incoming light is diffused, clear glazing may be used, enabling occupants to see clouds passing overhead,

and even stars at night. It must not be overlooked that larger glazing areas will incur increased winter heat losses, but except in the mildest climates, multiple glazing would be expected for museum skylights.

In its simplest form, a polar-oriented museum skylight is an architectural refinement of the sawtooth skylight, which was commonly used for single-storey industrial buildings in the first half of the twentieth century. Their polar-oriented characteristic is evident from the fact that, in the northern hemisphere, they were often referred to as 'northlight' roofs. Figure 4.53 shows a clean and simple adaptation of the sawtooth skylight at the Kroller-Muller Museum, and Figure 4.54 shows a more elaborate system that incorporates air-conditioning ducts and overhead maintenance catwalks at the Gulbenkian Modern Art Museum. The directional orientation of the glazing is evident, and in both cases, light-coloured surfaces are used to diffuse the overhead lighting and to soften what could otherwise be a noticeably strong lateral flow of light.

Polar-oriented skylights were central to the design concept for the Wallraf-Ricartz Museum. Figure 4.55 shows one section of the

Figure 4.54: *Polar-oriented skylights at the Gulbenkian Museum of Modern Art, Lisbon*

Figure 4.55: *Polar-oriented roof glazing with shading fins at the Wallraf-Rickartz Museum, Cologne*

skylights, facing north and tilted back towards south, and with shading fins on the mullions. Simply facing glazing north in the northern hemisphere does not ensure solar exclusion, as in summer the sun rises north of east and sets north of west, and the extent to which this occurs increases as latitude increases. These fins will cut out, or at least reduce, insolation during early summer mornings and evenings.

The pattern of the skylights at the Wallraf-Rickartz Museum has been developed by the designers as a highly visible design element. Figure 4.56 shows the stainless steel façade which proclaims to all visitors the outline of the skylight system, and this is reinforced by the interior design (Figure 4.57). These skylights continue over the smaller, individual galleries as well as over large gallery spaces (Figure 4.58), and throughout visitors are never lacking these visual statements of the origin of the lighting.

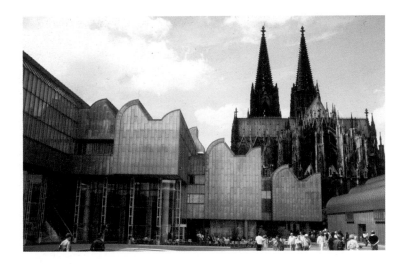

Figure 4.56: *Stainless steel façade reflecting the roof form of the polar-oriented skylight system at the Wallraf-Rickartz Museum*

Figure 4.57 *Architectural expression of the skylight system in an interior gallery space at the Wallraf-Rickartz Museum*

Figure 4.58: *A large gallery space, showing the skylight system and the diffused daylight that it provides at the Wallraf-Rickartz Museum*

The design of polar-oriented skylights is not intuitive, and some understanding of the underlying principles is necessary for appreciation of the design elements. For this, we will turn to the concept of the 'solar bracelet', but first we need to define a couple of terms.

- The solar equinoxes occur at the two points of the earth's orbit round the sun when earth's axis is at right angles to the sun's rays. They happen on or around 21 March and 21 September, and on these occasions at every unshaded location on earth, the sun rises due east and sets due west twelve hours later, giving equal night and day.

- The solar solstices occur at the two points where the earth's axis is at maximum tilt relative to the sun's rays. The tilt is the declination angle, and at the solstices has a value of approximately 23.5 degrees. For the northern hemisphere, the summer solstice happens on or around 21 June, and for the southern hemisphere, on or around 21 December.

Figure 4.59 shows the equinox and summer solstice sun paths for a northern hemisphere non-tropical location. At the equinoxes, the sun rises due east and six hours later reaches its peak altitude. At this point, the angle between the sun's rays and the zenith equals the latitude of the location. At the summer solstice, the sun's path is parallel to the plane of the equinox sun path, but displaced northwards through the declination angle of 23.5 degrees.

The solar bracelet is a stubby hollow cylinder that gives a 23.5 degree cut-off across its diameter, as shown in Figure 4.60. If the bracelet is held vertically and aligned on the east–west axis, and then is tilted towards the equator through the latitude angle, on mid-summer's day the rays of the rising sun will just penetrate to

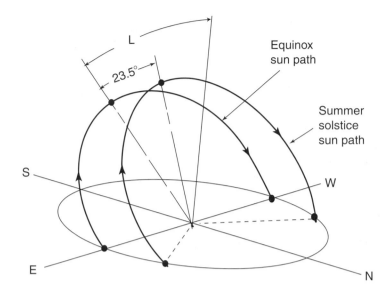

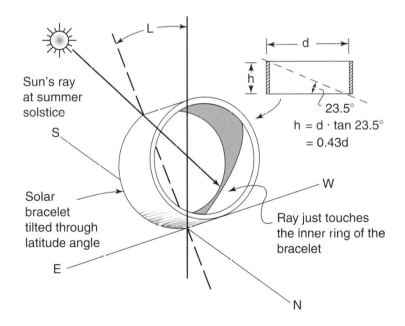

Figure 4.60: *The solar bracelet gives a cut-off equal to the solstice declination angle. If the bracelet is aligned on the east–west axis and tilted towards the equator through the latitude angle, it forms the optimum daylight-admitting fixed solar shading device*

the inner ring of the bracelet, and will continue to track around the perimeter of the inner ring throughout the day until sunset. In this way, the aperture of the bracelet is exposed to the great cone of polar-oriented sky that the sun never enters. If the building glazing is mounted in the plane of the inner ring, the bracelet is the optimally efficient form of external shading for admitting diffused light from the sky while maintaining total exclusion of direct sunlight. For more information on the solar bracelet, see Lynes and Cuttle (1988).

Figure 4.61: *Polar-oriented roof glazing sloped at the latitude angle, at the Waikato Art Museum, Hamilton, New Zealand*

Figure 4.62 *Square-cell aluminium louvre in the air gap of the double-glazing units gives the solstice declination angle cut-off, at the Waikato Art Museum*

Figure 4.63: *Skylights and fluorescent lighting at the Waikato Art Museum, with louvres below that are adjusted for seasonal variation of daylight availability*

Figure 4.64: *A gallery space at the Waikato Art Museum. Sunlight exclusion is not a problem, and visitors can look up through the louvres for a clear view of the sky*

The principle of the solar bracelet was applied in the design of the Waikato Art Museum, and Figure 4.61 shows the skylights which are oriented southwards, as the location has a latitude of 37.8°S, and tilted northwards through the latitude angle. At the equinoxes, the rays of the rising sun are parallel to the plane of the glazing and remain so throughout the day. The original proposal was to have an external shading grid, but cost considerations led to a shallow square-cell aluminium louvre between the panes of the double-glazing (Figure 4.62). The dimensions of the cells are such that one cell would exactly fit within a solar bracelet, that is to say, the diagonal cut-off angle is 23.5 degrees. A door at the end of each skylight opens into the plenum, which has a slotted catwalk and a simple installation of fluorescent lighting (Figure 4.63), and in the galleries below, louvres that are seasonally adjusted for illumination control are installed flush with the ceiling (Figure 4.64). Visitors can look up through the louvres and the clear-glazed skylights and see the sky.

Wall-lighting picture galleries

Samuel Hurst Seager, a New Zealand architect, enunciated the 'Top Side Lighting Method' for picture galleries in a paper published in the *Journal of the Royal Institute of British Architects* in 1912. Seager had toured many of the world's foremost art institutions and was strongly critical of what he had seen, claiming that 'No merchant would be willing to display his wares under such unfavourable conditions as were applied to many of the masterpieces in our art collections'. In his paper, he set out six principles for lighting picture galleries, and then proposed cross-sectional diagrams for two types of picture galleries, shown in Figures 4.65 and 4.66. His Top-Side Lighting (TSL) method is best known for these diagrams, and they deserve careful attention.

On the left-hand side of Figure 4.65, Seager shows how the distribution of illumination in galleries for large and medium-sized pictures is to be controlled. The skylight W-W comprises a type of glass that completely diffuses incident daylight, and for such a material the light intensity in a given direction inside the gallery will be proportional to the projected area of the skylight in that direction. Maximum intensity is directed to the bottom of the display wall, although this is not the zone of maximum illuminance because the upper wall is closer to the skylight, and this arrangement produces an illuminance distribution that achieves peak value around the mid-height of the picture hanging wall. Viewers

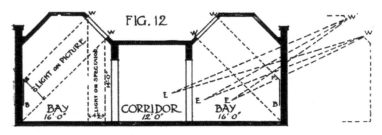

Figure 4.65: *Seager's Top-Side Lighting (TSL) proposal for medium- and large-size pictures*

adapt first to the relatively low light level in the corridor, and then as they turn into one of the lofty bays, they are faced by a wall washed with daylight. Within the hanging area the lighting is incident at an angle of approximately 45 degrees to the wall surface. These are the unique characteristics of Seager's TSL.

On the right-hand side, Seager has treated the display wall as a mirror surface and constructed the reflected image of the bay and its skylight. He shows three eye positions as a viewer catches a first glimpse from the corridor, moves into the bay, and examines a picture from closer range. In every case the reflected image appears above the hanging area, which means that providing the upper wall is given a matt finish, there will be an absence of veiling reflections.

The viewer's proximity to a painting is a crucial issue. Viewers can be expected to stand back from larger paintings, but they will want to move in closely to examine small paintings. The section shown in Figure 4.66 is better suited for small paintings. The maximum light intensity is incident at a steeper angle, in this case 55 degrees above the horizontal, allowing viewers to approach closer. The proximity of the upper wall to the skylight will ensure that in this case there will be a gradation of illuminance from the top of the wall to the bottom, but in a scaled-down gallery of this type, the top of the hanging area and the viewer's eye level will be relatively close to the top of the wall.

Soon after the paper was published, Seager was appointed sole assessor for an architectural competition for a new art gallery to be built in Wanganui, New Zealand. Seager took on the task with enthusiasm, and ensured that every competitor received a copy of his seminal paper. The Sarjeant Gallery, completed in 1917, epitomized the TSL method. From a central dome, two corridors lead to the bays (Figure 4.67), there being three bays on each side of each corridor (Figure 4.68). The first two bays are scaled for larger

Figure 4.66: *Seager's TSL proposal for small-size pictures*

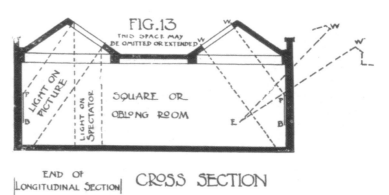

Figure 4.67: *Corridor leading to six daylit galleries at the Serjeant Gallery, Wanganui, New Zealand, designed in accordance with Seager's TSL proposal*

Figure 4.68: *The first two galleries on each side are for larger pictures, and the third gallery is less deep, and for medium-size pictures. Seager had intended that pictures would not be hung on the side walls, except that a small picture or two that could be hung adjacent to the corridor*

Figure 4.69: *Daylit gallery for small pictures at the Serjeant Gallery*

pictures, and the third for medium-size pictures. Actually, Seager had stipulated that just the first 1.5 m of the side walls may be used for small pictures, but otherwise these walls should be left blank. There were also two smaller galleries according to his other section (Figure 4.69).

Seager's proposals aroused much interest, and during the early 1920s he was invited to lecture in London and Paris, and his papers were reprinted in *American Architect*. In 1924, *The Builder* printed a diagram (Figure 4.70) by M. Bigot, the architect for the Musée Antoine Lécuyer, which was to be built in the war-shattered town of St Quentin, France. St Quentin's favourite son is Maurice-Quentin de La Tour, an eighteenth century pastellist who achieved fame for his portraits of French society, but the display of these works required special care. They are extremely fragile, and must be protected from vibration and movement as well as excessive light, while at the same time they need to be viewed at close range. Bigot's diagram is acknowledged to be based on a sketch by Seager, and clearly, it takes his ideas for close viewing a stage further than the Wanganui example. Full light intensity is maintained down to point B, and at point C there is a total cut-off of direct light from the skylight. The definition of this distribution will be affected by the reflectances of surface DE and its opposite surface, from the top of the skylight to the top of the wall. If these surfaces are dark, the distribution of light will be due to direct light from the skylight. If DE is lightened, there will be more light to the upper wall, and if the opposite surface is lightened, the cut-off around the bottom of the wall will be less pronounced. The reflected image of the skylight is well above the sightline even of

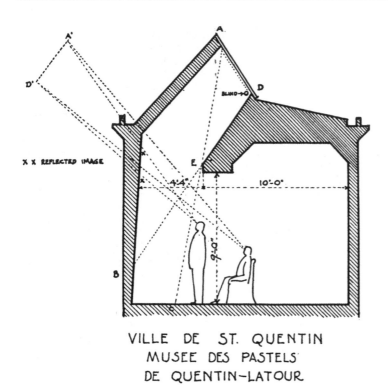

VILLE DE ST. QUENTIN
MUSEE DES PASTELS
DE QUENTIN-LATOUR

Section drawn by the Architect, M. BIGOT,
from sketch design by MR. S. HURST SEAGER.

the standing man who has approached to little more than 1 m from the display wall. Unfortunately, Bigot, who followed in the Beaux Arts tradition, chose not to adopt this approach for the Musée Antoine Lécuyer. Instead, he opted for central skylights, all of which have been subsequently blocked off, so that La Tour's pastels are now illuminated by indirect fluorescent lighting.

It is a fact that very little was actually built in accordance with Seager's proposals. There was a half-hearted effort to apply TSL in the Duveen Wing of the Tate Gallery in 1927, but it was far removed from Seager's principles and was never really satisfactory. The Robert McDougall Gallery (1930) in Seager's home town of Christchurch would seem to have been based on TSL, but in the 1950s the skylights were blanked off so that air-conditioning equipment could be installed in the roof spaces. More recently there has been another turn of events. The photographs shown of the Sarjeant Gallery were taken in the 1980s. Since then, the gallery lighting has been 'upgraded', which has involved replacing the skylight glazing with a material of such low transmittance that

Figure 4.71: *Perimeter wall lighting at the Musée de Moyen Age, Paris*

daylight is effectively eliminated on all but the very brightest summer days. The gallery is now illuminated by spotlights on lighting track, so that there is no longer an example of Seager's Top Side Lighting anywhere to be seen.

The most common approach to directed wall lighting may be described as the 'wall slot', and it is necessary to distinguish between this and perimeter daylighting. A very satisfactory example of perimeter daylighting can be seen at the Musée de Moyen Age (Museum of the Middle Ages) shown in Figure 4.71. Visitors to this hall have their attention immediately directed to the expanse of medieval, rough-textured wall and the carved figures displayed above the doorway. More carved figures are set on plinths in the strongly illuminated strip adjacent to the wall, where the downward flow of light reveals their features with strong shading patterns (Figure 4.72).

All too often, perimeter daylighting is reduced to such a narrow strip that the result is quite unsatisfactory, particularly for displaying pictures. The viewer is confronted with a strongly illuminated upper wall, and a strip of relatively strongly illuminated floor adjacent to the wall, with a line of poorly lit pictures hanging

Figure 4.72: *Detail of the effect of the perimeter wall lighting on the textured wall surface and the sculptured heads, at the Musée de Moyen Age*

between these two zones. The downward flow of light strongly illuminates the tops of the picture frames, often causing a visible flash of reflected light on the wall above the frames, while the visible surface of the upper frame member is not only in shadow, but casts a shadow over some, or even all, of the picture. The lower frame member is the brightest element in the field of view, and casts its shadow onto the wall below the picture. To this is added the dismal effect of every defect in the wall surface being starkly revealed, causing an overall effect that is, in my experience, never satisfactory for displaying pictures. I do not wish to embarrass any museum by illustrating the shortcomings of the wall slot, but this architectural detail has been reproduced so many times that readers should have little difficulty in finding an example where they can make their own assessment of this misapplication of daylighting.

It is a real architectural challenge to achieve wall-directed daylighting in picture galleries without intruding unduly into the space. Figure 4.70 shows how a controlled distribution of wall illumination could be achieved in a situation where viewers approach close to the wall, and the ceiling is brought down to just above their heads. Simply scaling up this solution does not work, because the viewer's eye level does not change and we are left with just another wall-slot installation and all the defects that go with that approach. However, there have been some notable efforts to incorporate architectural elements into the roofs of galleries with the aim of directing the incoming daylight away from the middle of the space and onto the walls.

Figure 4.73: *Aalto's wall lighting system at the Nordijllands Kunstmuseum, Aalborg, Denmark*

Figure 4.74: *One of the central wall lighting reflectors at the Nordijllands Kunstmuseum*

At the Nordijllands Kunstmuseum, Alvar Aalto achieved a controlled distribution of wall-directed daylighting by means of a suspended four-sided reflector (Figure 4.73). Within the opening of a clear-glazed central skylight, the suspended element has curved, matt-white reflecting surfaces on four sides, which both wash the hanging walls with reflected light and shield the viewing positions from direct light (Figure 4.74). The viewing conditions at the time of my visit were very satisfactory, although it would appear that at some times of the year shafts of sunlight might penetrate in to the gallery at the corners of the skylight (Figure 4.75). Also, it should be noted that these galleries would not be able to accommodate large paintings. Furthermore, I have to add this level of light control has not been achieved without a sense of intrusion into the gallery space. I felt a sense of unease in these galleries. It was as if vast steam hammers were poised to descend Conan Doyle style to crush the occupants. While I am not claustrophobic by nature, I felt this to be a very enclosed space which is not altogether conducive to enjoying the experience of a daylit space.

An alternative approach to controlling the daylight distribution is to construct a ceiling of baffles, and an example of this is shown in Figure 4.76. There is a problem with ceiling baffles. It needs to be understood that they do not redirect light in the way that polished metal reflectors do. Only the incoming daylight that is travelling in the wanted directions passes through the baffles without interception, and for this to be the only light admitted, the baffles would have to be matt black. This would both reduce the amount of daylight entering the space and would give a very unattractive appearance to the ceiling. As is shown in Figure 4.76, it is usual for baffles to be painted matt white, with the effect that much of the

Figure 4.76: *Wall lighting ceiling baffles at the Louvre, Paris*

directional control of the light is lost. Additional light is gained by adding a diffusely reflected component to the directional component, and it can be seen that the walls are indeed well lit, but so is the central part of the floor.

Two extensions to the Tate Gallery, London, have shown differing approaches to providing wall-directed daylighting. The first of these opened in 1979, and comprises a 63 × 27 m space that is spanned by a roof comprising twenty-one 9 × 9 m bays (Figures 4.77–4.79). The beams which form the edges of the bays carry the air-conditioning services and enable the space to be subdivided by display panels. Each bay supports a pyramid skylight, above which is a two-level motorized louvre, and beneath which is a deep baffle structure (Figure 4.79). The baffles are unpainted, and the grey tone of the concrete is partially effective in achieving wall-directed lighting. The square enclosure at the

Figure 4.77: *A roof of deep baffles forming square bays at the Tate Gallery, London*

Figure 4.78: *The roof beams at the Tate Gallery incorporate air ducts, and provide for dividing the space with display walls*

Figure 4.79: *Motorized louvres control daylight from a pyramid skylight, and baffles give directional control. Spotlights are supplementing the daylight, and the central fixture provides night time illumination. Tate Gallery, London*

centre of the baffles shields daylight from the middle of the bay, and houses fluorescent lamps to provide ambient illumination when daylight is insufficient. Lighting track around the perimeter of the enclosure supports spotlights which, as shown in the figures, may be used to supplement wall illumination during daylight hours.

This installation is notable for its electronic controls. The designers had taken the trouble to provide exhibitions designers with a variety of control options, so that a range of light levels could be set, such as 100–200 lux, and the control system would adjust the louvres for each bay only when the light level approached one end of the range. The intention was that viewers would be conscious of light level fluctuations, which they would associate with the everyday experience of daylight illumination. Some differences of opinion have been expressed as to whether or not this intention has been satisfied. Certainly, the control options did provide for preset light levels to be maintained within tight limits by continuous adjustment of the overhead louvres, and, initially at least, it seems that this was the control option that the museum staff favoured.

The other extension is the Clore Gallery, which opened in 1987. The ceilings comprise deep baffles without active controls, and as shown in Figure 4.80, substantial diversities of daylight illumination may occur within a gallery space that can quite overwhelm the electric lighting. Peter Wilson, Curator of the Tate Gallery, has explained the south-facing non-motorized louvres were set for sunlight exclusion, and the north-facing louvres for a 'scooping effect'. Even so, it was intended that the balance of lighting within the galleries should respond to seasonal and diurnal variations in outdoor daylight, and that there could be distinctly different

Figure 4.80: *Angled skylights provide diurnal variation of daylight distribution at the Clore Gallery, Tate Gallery, London*

Figure 4.81: *Viewing booths enable visitors to enjoy the views across the River Thames with minimal interference to the adaptation level within the gallery, at the Clore Gallery*

viewing experiences viewing the galleries in the morning or the afternoon of the same day. Furthermore, this gallery was built to house the Tate's collection of paintings by J.M.W. Turner, who often painted views across the River Thames. The Clore Gallery is adjacent to the Thames, and to enable viewers to make this connection without sacrificing large expanses of hanging wall or creating visual adaptation problems, small, partially enclosed spaces with angled windows giving extensive views across the river have been incorporated into some galleries (Figure 4.81).

This is a gallery that provides directed wall lighting, which is not a naturally occurring daylight condition, but in which viewers are quite conscious that they are experiencing the galleries illuminated

Figure 4.82: *Directed wall lighting that varies with changing outdoor conditions at the Clore Gallery*

by daylight (Figure 4.82). The carefully contrived visual connections to the outdoors play their part, but also the policy of allowing illuminance on the paintings to swing within ranges has contributed to this aim. This does not mean that conservation concerns have been abandoned. The policy at the Clore Gallery is to maintain exposure within cumulative annual limits rather than to maintain a constant limiting illuminance value.

The presence of daylight

All of the foregoing daylighting typologies have been devised with the intention that daylight is to be the source of illumination by which the artworks are seen. In this final section, we look at some examples of daylighting where this may not have been the intention, or at least, was not a primary design objective.

The villa of Louisiana, to the north of Copenhagen, had been used for art displays for some years when, in 1958, Jorgen Bo and Wilhelm Wohlert transformed the villa into a unique art gallery. They added glazed corridors which wind through the extensive gardens that contain strategically positioned sculptures, and which connect a series of pavilions, each offering a different setting

Figure 4.83: *Glazed walkways through the gardens connecting pavilions at the Louisiana Gallery, Humelbaek, Denmark, on a summer afternoon*

Figure 4.84: *The walkways on a winter afternoon, at the Louisiana Gallery*

in which to display art. I have visited the Louisiana Museum for Modern Art twice, once on a warm, sunny day in August, and again on a cold, overcast afternoon in early January. Figures 4.83 to 4.90 are my photographs from these two visits arranged in pairs to contrast the two experiences.

Figures 4.85 and 4.86: *Summer and winter views inside the walkways at the Louisiana Gallery*

There is no attempt here to optimize viewing conditions, or to provide every visitor with a preconceived visual experience. Every visit to this gallery will be a unique event, with the context of season, time of day, and the vagaries of the weather being as much part of the experience as the gallery spaces themselves. This is a gallery that invites one to come back again, to see art quite literally in a different light. There may be times when sun

Figures 4.87 and 4.88: *Summer and winter views in one of the pavilions at the Louisiana Gallery*

glare will make viewing difficult from some positions, or when mist will obscure the surroundings, but these will be overwhelmed in memory by the serendipitous occasions.

In 1971 the City of Glasgow initiated an architectural competition for a museum to house the world-class collection of art connoisseur Sir Willam Burrell, which had been donated to the city in

Figures 4.89 and 4.90: *Summer and winter views from one of the gallery spaces at the Louisiana Gallery*

1944, together with funds for the museum. The site was a country park on the edge of the city which contained a large meadow surrounded by woodland. Most of the competitors placed their proposed buildings in the middle of this meadow, but one group located their building adjacent to the woodland. Their aim was to achieve an interwoven relationship between art and nature, and as the project architect Barry Gasson has described, to include 'a walk in the woods' in the primary route through the building. Visitors pass through a series of medieval stone archways that Burrell had collected to enter a space with extensive north-facing glazing that connects directly to the woodland, as shown in Figure 4.91.

This view was taken on a summer day, when the sunlight and the breeze combined to create continually changing patterns of dappled light and shade. In winter, this deciduous woodland would give views through to the northern sky, and sometimes there would be the shadow patterns of the bare trees cast onto a snow-covered landscape by the low altitude sun. This area is reserved for displays of materials that are non-responsive to light

Figure 4.91: *Gasson's 'Walk in the woods' at the Burrell Collection, Glasgow, UK*

Figure 4.92: *One of the skylit walkways that connect through the Burrell Collection*

exposure, such as ceramics and bronze, but glazed walkways (Figure 4.92) from this area connect to spaces deeper within the building where light levels can be controlled within closer limits. The visitor is presented with a choice of following a walkway or entering one of the enclosed gallery spaces, as shown in Figure 4.93.

There are many ways in which daylight may be an integral component of the museum viewing experience, without necessarily being the prime source of illumination for the objects on display. The Orangerie Museum is illuminated by electric lighting, but it is located in the Tuileries Gardens and visitors are kept aware of this setting. Substantial areas of potential hanging space are sacrificed for windows which, as at the Burrell, rely on adjacent deciduous foliage for brightness control (Figure 4.94). At the Dallas Museum of Art, architect Larrabee Barnes has created a cathedral-like space for large, modern artworks, and these objects

Figure 4.93: *A choice of taking the walkway, or entering one of the enclosed gallery spaces at the Burrell Collection*

Figure 4.94: *The galleries at l'Orangerie, Paris, have fluorescent lighting, and also a strong sense of connection with the outdoors*

are lit by adjustable spotlights. In this setting, a single slot of high-level glazing showing a narrow slice of Texan sky has an impact quite out of proportion to its size (Figure 4.95).

While Louis Kahn was working on the design of the Kimbell Art Museum, he stated his intention that 'the light in the rooms structured in concrete will have the luminosity of silver'. When the design drawings were released, there was consternation among lighting experts. They insisted that his design would not work. The 740 mm wide strip of glazing was quite insufficient for 7 m wide gallery spaces, and as if that was not enough, immediately

Figure 4.95: *The slot in the wall that gives a view of bright sky has an impact that is out of proportion with its size, at the Dallas Fine Arts Museum, Dallas, Texas*

beneath each of these strips was a pair of linear, concave reflectors made of perforated aluminium that would direct almost all of the incoming light onto the underside surfaces of the roof vaults. The result would be that the artworks would be hopelessly underlit. Some of these experts suggested that Kahn should be reminded that visitors to the museum were not there to see his structural concrete, but to see the art.

It takes a visit to the Kimbell to convince that Kahn, working with lighting designer Richard Kelly, knew what he was doing. While I will not be persuaded to offer a definition of 'the luminosity of silver', I willingly concede that Kahn got it. Entering on a bright sunny day, one is conscious of the glow of light overhead, despite the strong flow of light from the glazed entrance doors (Figure 4.96). Moving on to the galleries, that glow remains as attention is drawn to the surrounding artworks (Figure 4.97). Kahn's 'natural lighting fixture' comprises a pair of 30 m long clear-span concrete shells, and a facing pair of finely perforated aluminium reflectors under the clear polycarbonate-glazed slot between the shells (Figure 4.98). The shells are washed with reflected daylight, and at their ends a thin strip of glass separates them from the structure, suggesting that they are floating without support. I have heard that numerous concrete samples with slightly differing blends of colouring materials had to be mixed and cast for Kahn's inspection before he gave his approval. The end result is a unique setting for art (Figure 4.99).

On one occasion I met Larry Eubank, who looks after the lighting at the Kimbell, and as we sat in his office he explained the museum's lighting policy. Although it was a Monday and the gallery was closed to the public, we then wandered through some

Figure 4.96: *Kahn's 'luminosity of silver' at the Kimbell Art Museum, Fort Worth, Texas*

Figure 4.97: *Daylight entering through a narrow slot is reflected up onto the concrete ceiling vaults, while electric lighting illuminates the artworks at the Kimbell Art Museum*

Figure 4.98: *Detail of the ceiling vaults separated from the walls by a glass strip, giving the appearance of floating, at the Kimbell Art Museum*

Figure 4.99 *The lighting at the Kimbell Art Museum is achieved by a balance the daylighting and electric lighting systems*

of the gallery spaces. The electric lighting was off, and I was quite startled by what I saw (Figure 4.100). I measured the illuminance on the pictures, and although it was early afternoon and it was a bright sunny day, the values were between 60 and 65 lux. I asked Larry to switch on the electric lighting, and the values shot up to between 180 and 240 lux. In other words, the daylight illumination onto the pictures was between one quarter and one third of the total illumination. It would be interesting to see the galleries at night-time, but it appears that that the museum does not normally open for evening viewing. It is easy to speculate that the reason for this may be that just as the electric lighting is essential for viewing, so too is the daylight glow of Kahn's 'natural lighting fixture'.

I understand that since my visit the electric lighting at the Kimbell has been modified. The original design by Richard Kelly was all mains voltage PAR38 incandescent filament lighting with a colour temperature of 2800K, and inevitably there was a noticeable difference of colour appearance between the daylight and electric lighting. Perhaps with the aim of reducing this difference, I understand that museum staff are making increasing use of low voltage halogen lamps with colour temperatures around 3200K. Certainly, the original installation would have been very energy-inefficient by today's standards, which is another good reason for change.

Before leaving this topic, we will take a look at Kahn's last project, the Yale Center for British Art, which was completed after his death in 1974. In this case he had a constricted site in the city of New Haven, and his solution was a four-storey building with two courtyards that penetrate from roof down to ground level.

Figure 4.101: *View from a top floor gallery at the Yale Center for British Art, New Haven, Connecticut, into a sunlit-enclosed courtyard*

The roof-level glazing system allows sunlight to stream through into the courtyards, which are linked to the galleries by large, unglazed apertures (Figure 4.101). However, the glazing over the top floor galleries diffuses direct sunlight and directs daylight preferentially onto the display surfaces (Figure 4.102). Open apertures to the courtyards are repeated at lower gallery floors, and although the artworks at these levels are illuminated entirely by electric lighting, Kahn maintains a distinct sense of connection to daylight through these apertures (Figure 4.103). Once again, Kahn has used daylight more as a source of reference than as a source of illumination.

For all of the previous sections in this chapter, the daylighting design objectives have been reasonably clear and straightforward. The discussion of 'the presence of daylight' in this section raises more questions than it answers. What is the role of daylight in a daylit gallery? Is it that viewers experience the artworks illuminated by daylight, or that the gallery is lit by daylight, and not necessarily the art? Is it an illumination issue, or is it one of visual contact? Is the issue whether or not viewers feel themselves to be in contact with nature and the outdoor world while they are looking at an indoor display of art? While it would seem pointless to expect that there is a unique answer to these questions, it probably

Figure 4.102: *A top floor gallery at the Yale Center for British Art, showing diffused daylight from the prismatic skylights over the gallery spaces*

is true that a designer needs to ask these questions to have a clear sense of purpose.

Finally, there are practical issues involved in connecting viewers with daylight. Although the examples illustrated in this section might appear to have been quite simply achieved, this is not the case. Kjeld Kjeldsen, Director of the Louisiana Museum of Modern Art, told me that 'the art galleries of the future will be designed by insurance companies'. The glazed pathway through the gardens connecting isolated pavilions cannot be used for visiting exhibitions.

Figure 4.103: *A second floor level gallery, with electric lighting and visual connection to one of the four storeys high enclosed courtyards, at the Yale Center for British Art*

The level of security provided is quite insufficient to satisfy the insurers, and furthermore, the level of environmental control is insufficient to satisfy the lenders. New galleries, securely enclosed and air-conditioned, have been added onto the site, and these are used for all visiting exhibitions. Inevitably, they lack those distinctive qualities that make a visit to the Louisiana such a memorable occasion.

Barry Gasson's 'walk in the woods' also alarmed the insurance companies, but in this case the issue was resolved before construction started. They were concerned not merely about a burglar sneaking in through the windows, but the possibility that a truck might be driven through the glazed wall that opens to the woodland. The solution was to install massive panels inside the glass line that are raised by hydraulic rams every night. Occasionally some of the rams malfunction, and a panel or two may remain stranded during daytime (Figure 4.104).

Kahn's insistence that the apertures linking the galleries to the courtyards at the Yale Center for British Art must be unglazed aroused the concerns of the local fire officers, as this would permit fire spread between floors. The solution was to install fire-rated shutters that will automatically descend to close the apertures in the event of fire. Visitors who approach the apertures are confronted by prominent signs advising them stand back, and definitely not to lean through the apertures, when the fire alarm sounds. Enabling viewers to experience the presence of daylight can turn out to be more difficult than it might at first seem.

Figure 4.104: *One of the heavy security panels at the Burrell Collection that has failed to retract below floor level*

Daylighting controls

5

The previous chapter covered a number of different architectural approaches to controlling the admission and redistribution of daylight in art galleries and museums. Generally these involved the orientation and slope of the glazing; sometimes they have incorporated external or internal shading or other light control devices. The features of the systems that have been described varied substantially in complexity, some involving multiple glazing systems with special transmission properties, and others having active controls to regulate light admission. In this chapter we review glazing options and the opportunities that they offer for daylight control, including some materials and glazing systems that have not, as far as I am aware, ever been used in museums. As the previous chapter has looked back at past efforts to enable visitors to experience museums in daylight, the aim of this chapter is to look ahead to some of the emerging technologies, and to consider what they might have to offer for museum lighting.

Light transmission

Glass is an amorphous solid, being hard and brittle like a solid while possessing other physical properties of a liquid. While there are many different formulations of glass for specialized purposes, soda-lime glass is the most common type of glass, and it is this glass that is commonly used for window glazing. The components are silica from sand, lime from heated limestone, and sodium carbonate, otherwise known as washing soda. These ingredients fuse into glass inside a furnace at a temperature of 1700°C, after which it flows as a glowing liquid onto molten tin inside a float bath, and is drawn off at 600°C as a continuous ribbon of clear glass. It then undergoes controlled cooling as it passes through an annealing lehr, before it is ready for cutting.

Light is lost in transmission through a pane of clear glass by two processes: reflection and absorption. Reflection at glass surfaces is discussed in the following chapter in relation to avoiding unwanted reflections in picture or display case glazing. Absorption losses are due mainly to impurities in the glass, and for optical

Facing page: Museum of Contemporary Art, Los Angeles, California

fibres, where light may be required to travel long distances in glass, very high standards of purity are obtained. For window glazing, where the light has to travel only a few millimetres in glass, less rigorous standards are applied. The principal source of contamination is iron impurities which commonly occur in sand. Pure silica sand is white, and is quite rare in nature. The much more familiar golden sand gains its colour from ferric oxide impurities, and when used in glass manufacture, the visible result is a green tint in the body of the glass. For the 3 and 5 mm thick glass panes that are used in domestic windows, the effect on the colour of transmitted light is imperceptible. Where thicker glass is used for larger panes, or for multiple glazing systems, the colour may be noticeable, particularly if there is an opportunity for comparison with an unglazed view to the outside. There are contrasting opinions about this effect. If there is no opportunity for comparison, so that viewers undergo chromatic adaptation to the prevailing illumination, they are unlikely to notice the green tint. However, some are not convinced by this argument, and make the counter proposition that the whole point of providing daylight in a museum is to enable visitors to experience the exhibits under the light in which human vision has evolved, and so the museum is obliged to provide that light without distortion. To accommodate this view, several glass manufacturers offer a 'white' low-iron glass as an alternative to common soda-lime glass, but this option comes with a significant price tag. Figure 5.1 compares the spectral transmittance curves for several window glass types.

Situations occur where some reduced light transmission is wanted. Where there is a view from a gallery with restricted illumination through to the outdoors or to some other brighter space, reduced transmission glass may be used to balance brightness within the gallery. Body tinted glass is produced by metal oxides being added to the melt, enabling a range of colours, including grey. Once a furnace has been turned over to a particular colour, glass will be drawn off in different thicknesses, so that the density of the colour increases with glass thickness. While a grey body tinted glass of appropriate density may provide for a satisfactory appearance of the view to the brighter space, it should not be assumed that the light coming from that space will be spectrally undistorted. If that light is to illuminate exhibits for which colour appearance is important, it will be necessary to assess the effect of the spectral transmittance distribution of the glass on colour rendering.

There are many other variations of clear glass. Patterned, fritted, or sandblasted glass may be used to diffuse incoming light, and prismatic glass may be used to deflect light by refraction. Coatings

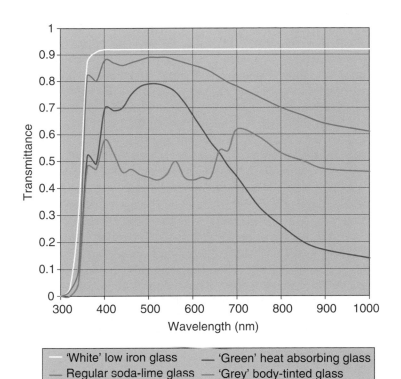

Figure 5.1: *Spectral transmittance curves for several types of window glass*

on glass can substantially affect glazing properties. Also, clear plastics, such as acrylic (polymerized methylmethacrylate or PMMA) and polycarbonate, are widely used for display cases, but not for window glazing except when certain properties, such as UV blocking or light deflection, are required. In such cases, they may be added as separate panes inside the glazing.

The previous chapter illustrates a variety of uses of adjustable blinds and louvres to control indoor daylight levels. Particularly where there is a conservation need to control daylight, photoelectric monitoring devices may be used to control the operation of motorized blinds or louvres. Glazing materials having variable light transmission would seem to be the next step, and there have been significant advances in the technology of such materials.

We are familiar with spectacle lenses that darken when the wearer steps outside, so it may be asked, why is this type of material not used for museum lighting? These lenses are photochromic materials, which darken when exposed to ultraviolet radiation. Generally the darkening response to exposure is rapid, and clearing after exposure takes longer. Unfortunately the materials that clear more rapidly tend to fail more rapidly, so that after repeated exposures, clearing becomes incomplete and one is left with glazing that never returns to its clear state. Even if it were practical to manufacture such materials in windowpane sizes, to then mount them on rooftops where they are fully exposed to the sun and sky would ensure a short life. A quite different technology that does have potential for practical application is electrochromic glazing. A microscopically thin coating on clear glass can control the light transmission over a large range by application of a low voltage, and then reversing the voltage clears the glazing. Windows employing this technology are currently available, but generally they take on a distinct colour as they darken. Electrochromic glazing that imparts no significant colour effects, and with light transmission controlled by a photoelectric monitoring device, may become a practical reality for museums. For more information on glazing performance, see Button and Pye (1993).

Light distribution

The previous chapter illustrates various architectural forms that have been developed with the aim of controlling the distribution of light in museums, particularly in picture galleries. In this section we will review some recent applications and technologies for controlling daylight distribution in buildings, some of which might find applications in museums. For more information on the technologies described, refer to IEA (2000).

Light shelves

This simple device comprises a horizontal reflector which intercepts daylight that would otherwise produce a band of strong illumination adjacent to the window, and redirects it onto the ceiling to provide diffused daylight over a greater depth into the space. If the incoming light is diffused light from the sky, it makes no difference whether the reflecting surface is specular or matt, as long as high reflectance is maintained. In sunny conditions, a specular reflector can deflect a beam of sunlight across the upper surfaces of the space, but this effect is dependent on the sun's position and the state of the weather. For any space where the aim is to achieve a reasonably consistent daylight distribution, a matt reflector surface would be advisable. It would also be necessary to examine solar incidence to ensure that display areas are protected.

Basically similar effects can be achieved by horizontal louvres with reflective upper surfaces, and again, sunlight incidence must be examined carefully. It is unlikely that this approach will be satisfactory where moderately or highly light-responsive materials may be displayed, or for east- or west-oriented façades. The design principle is that the horizontal devices act both as reflectors and as shading elements, and that restricts the opportunities for application.

Light deflectors

A variety of materials and glazing systems has been developed for this purpose, the general principles being shown in Figure 5.2. Prismatic glass panels have been used for many years to deflect incoming daylight up onto the ceiling and upper room surfaces, and while they can be quite effective for deflecting high altitude skylight upwards, they do not provide well for view to the outside. Recent developments have made available other ways of achieving this effect.

Laser-cut panels are thin panels of clear acrylic that have been divided into arrays of rectangular elements by laser cutting. The result is like a miniaturized louvre blind, and like a blind, the 'blades' may be normal to or inclined to the plane of the panel, the difference being that this is not adjustable. Light that is incident parallel to the 'blades' passes through the panel with minimal interruption, and provides a reasonably clear view through the

Light from high altitude, which may
be sunlight or overhead skylight, is
deflected upwards onto the ceiling

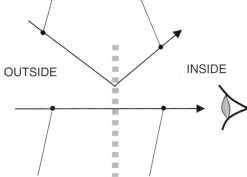

OUTSIDE   INSIDE

Light from low altitude passes through to
give external view

Figure 5.2: *The roles of light deflectors*

panel. For light incident obliquely, the 'blades' act as fairly efficient specular reflectors, and laser-cut panels attached as inner panes to side windows can provide a useful redistribution of incoming light. They have the advantages of being much lighter than prismatic glass and being easier to maintain than louvres, while providing relatively uninterrupted view. They can also be applied in skylights to spread incoming light outwards towards the walls.

Shaped clear acrylic strips, or metal louvre blades, in some cases with mirror finishes, can be stacked within double-glazed units to deflect incoming daylight. These permit little or no view through, but again, they can deflect daylight from side windows that normally would be incident on a narrow strip adjacent to the wall, onto the ceiling, and in so doing, greatly increase the depth of useful daylight illumination in the space.

Holographic optical elements (HOEs) are diffraction gratings formed on thin plastic film which is embedded in a glass laminate. Among their useful properties is the selective nature of their reflection and transmission characteristics. They can be set to provide transparent shading, so that from inside a building there is a relatively uninterrupted view, while incident sunlight from higher angles is reflected. HOEs may also be used in conjunction with other devices, such as the shaped acrylic strips described in the previous paragraph, to improve overall performance.

Light ducts

One of the earliest examples of a light duct lined with reflective film to transport daylight to a location inside a building occurred at the National Gallery of Canada. Architect Moshe Safdie wanted to have two floors of daylit galleries. For the upper floor he decided upon a central skylight in a barrel-vault ceiling, fitted with a prismatic panel that refracted some of the light onto the walls. To achieve a similar effect on the floor below, he staggered the arrangement of galleries on the two floors so that he could locate vertical shafts between the upper floor galleries to coincide with the central skylights of the galleries below. The effect in a lower floor gallery is shown in Figure 5.3, and so proud was Safdie of his invention, that visitors passing between upper floor galleries can peer through portholes into the light ducts for the intriguing view of multiple reflections shown in Figure 5.4. The ducts are lined with aluminized mylar film, and this photograph was taken when the film was quite new. It was evident on a more recent visit to the

Figure 5.3: A lower floor gallery with central skylight at the National Gallery of Canada, Ottawa, Canada. The skylight is connected to roof level by a light duct

gallery that this material had deteriorated and was in need of replacement.

There are commercially available systems of 'light pipes' which generally comprise a lightweight cylindrical steel duct with reflective internal lining connecting an external input and an internal output fixture. Usually the aim is to capture as much direct sunlight as possible, so that in temperate climates the output is very variable. Much more consistent performance could be achieved by polar orientation of the input fixture (see Chapter 4, p. 91), but a large duct diameter might be required to gather sufficient daylight. An anidolic reflector offers the prospect of being able to concentrate diffuse light from a selected portion of the sky, and transmit that light to another anidolic reflector where it will be 'deconcentrated' and diffused within an interior space.

Figure 5.5 shows the principle of the anidolic reflector, where point D is the focal point of the parabolic contour that passes through C and A, and the axis of this contour is indicated by the chain dotted line. It follows that any ray that passes through D to

Figure 5.4: *At the upper gallery level, visitors can peer through a port hole into the light ducts for this strange view. The National Gallery of Canada*

Figure 5.5: *The anidolic reflector. Light entering the smaller aperture of the reflector emerges from the larger aperture contained within the acceptance cone. In reverse, light gathered from within the acceptance cone at the larger aperture undergoes concentration to emerge from the smaller aperture*

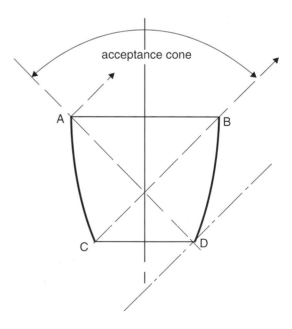

be incident on the reflector between A and C will be reflected parallel to this axis. Similarly, point C is the focal point for the reflector contour BD, so that any ray that enters the reflector between C and D will emerge within the acceptance cone shown, whether directly or after reflection. As all rays in optics are reversible, it follows that any ray from within the acceptance cone that enters the anidolic reflector through the aperture AB emerges through the smaller aperture CD. In this way, the larger aperture of an anidolic reflector may be tilted towards the polar-oriented cone of sunless sky (see Figure 4.59), and employed to concentrate the diffused incoming sky light into the input end a light pipe of smaller diameter. The light pipe may connect to the smaller aperture of a second anidolic reflector at the output end of the light pipe, which acts to 'deconcentrate' the daylight into the indoor space, while containing it within the acceptance cone. The angular size of the acceptance cone and the degree of concentration achieved depend upon the tilt angle chosen for the axes of the parabolic contours.

Ultraviolet transmission

The CIE divides the UV portion of the electromagnetic spectrum into three regions: UV-C is 100–280 nm; UV-B is 280–315 nm; and UV-A is 315–400 nm. The solar spectrum measured outside the earth's atmosphere has radiant power at all UV wavelengths. The upper layers of the atmosphere effectively protect us from UV-C radiation, and protection from this radiation is essential for all forms of life on this planet. The photon energies in this band of short-wavelength radiation are high, and UV-C radiation is damaging to all types of living tissues. The UV-B range reaches the earth's surface, and is responsible for the erythemal or sun-tanning effect on exposed skin. It can also cause serious skin damage, such as melanomas, and it would be a very potent source of damage if it ever reached light-responsive museum objects. UV-A is relatively abundant in the solar spectrum at ground level, and also it passes through glass. In fact, the reason why the CIE set the limit at 315 nm is because soda-lime glass is effectively opaque to all radiation of shorter wavelengths. We should note that common glass, whether for window glazing, display cases or picture glazing, is protecting museum objects from UV-B radiation. The long wavelength end of the UV-A range causes some difficulty, as the CIE defines the short-wavelength end of the visible spectrum as occurring at 380 nm, so that there is a 20 nm overlap of the visible and UV spectra. The difficulty comes from the fact that some manufacturers of UV filters make claims for the performance of their products, treating only radiation of wavelengths shorter than 380 nm as UV, whereas most museum conservators consider any radiation of wavelengths shorter than 400 nm to be UV.

If we take the attitude that all radiation of wavelengths less than 400 nm is unwanted, there is a variety of ways to achieve this. An ideal glazing material would have zero transmittance below 400 nm, above which point it would switch to having the transmittance of clear glass. While such a material would block the visible 20 nm waveband 380–400 nm, the visual response at this far-violet end of the visible spectrum is very low and the visual effect of this loss may be disregarded. Unfortunately, it is technically difficult to achieve a rapid switch from absorbing to transmitting functions. Special formulations of glass can achieve high levels of UV blocking, but they tend also to partially block the shorter visible wavelengths, and the visible effect of this is to give the transmitted light a yellowish tint. UV blocking plastics, particularly acrylics, have been more successful in achieving effective UV control without unwanted colour effects, and these are often used for display cabinets. For window glazing, laminated glass using UV blocking plastic interlayers can be very successful. These materials can receive very heavy UV exposure, and plastics are likely to degrade quite rapidly when used in this way. Laminated plastic interlayers, usually poly vinyl butyrate (PVB), benefit by being protected from contact with oxygen. Even so, it is always beneficial for UV blocking plastics to be installed so that they are shaded from direct sunlight. The sharpest transmittance switchover at 400 nm is obtained by dichroic coatings, and filters employing this technology are discussed in Chapter 7 as they are widely used with display spotlights. So far, this technology is not used for window glazing.

Solar heat gain

A daylighting strategy inevitably involves significant areas of glazing, and while this is not strictly a lighting issue, the effect of solar heat gains cannot be overlooked when daylighting systems are being considered. Gains can be reduced by use of solar control glasses and many varieties have been used in commercial buildings, but in these applications some spectral modification of the admitted light is tolerated or even seen to be an attractive feature. Almost half of incident solar power is infrared radiation, and a solar control glass that blocks the IR while admitting daylight without spectral effect would be an ideal option for museums. Unfortunately it is technically difficult to achieve this. Body tinted glazing usually reduces light transmission more than IR, giving a low light/heat ratio, with the most notable exception being glass that has a high iron content (Figure 5.1). This glass is readily identified by its distinctly green appearance, which makes it unsuitable for all applications where colour appearance is important.

More favourable light/heat ratios can be achieved by using glazing with reflective coatings. Coatings that are applied on-line are called pyrolitic coatings as they are applied onto the surface of the glass while it is still hot and passing through the annealing lehr. These are hard coatings, and after application, the glass can be cut and worked, which may include bending, drilling or edge polishing. Off-line coatings are applied after cutting and other working of the glass, and may involve dipping panes into chemical solutions and firing the glass to make the coatings durable, or alternatively, vacuum deposition. This process involves placing glass panes in a chamber which is evacuated to a high level of vacuum, and then sputtering a metal inside the chamber. The metal becomes the cathode in a high-voltage electrical circuit, and the molecules that are driven from its surface, instead of forming droplets as would happen in air, disperse as a fine mist which settles on surrounding surfaces. The control of this process has been improved by the recent development of magnetron sputtering, and the result is that thin metallic coatings with a variety of reflection and transmission properties can be produced. However, these coatings are fragile, so that all working of the glass must be completed before coating, and the coating must be protected either by laminating or by forming into a multiple glazing unit.

The popularity of reflective coatings in commercial buildings is due not only to their thermal performance but also to the shiny and often colourful appearance that they contribute to building façades. These visible effects are not necessary, for by controlling the coating thickness, glazing performance can be tailored to affect selected spectral wavebands. Low E glass utilizes ultra thin metallic coatings which may affect IR and UV transmission without visible effect. The emissivity for uncoated glass is 0.9, and this can be reduced to around 0.1 by a low E coating, resulting in the IR reflectance increasing to more than 0.8. Such coatings may be applied by either on-line or off-line processes to give glasses that may appear indistinguishable from clear glass while significantly reducing solar heat gains. Hard coatings as well as soft coatings may be incorporated into multiple glazing units to give improved thermal insulation performance.

Thermal transmission

Insulation is another aspect of glazing performance that cannot be overlooked. It is important in museums not merely for energy conservation, but because close control of air temperature and relative humidity requires that surface temperature variations are minimized. Also, condensation forming on cool surfaces can cause serious damage in a museum, particularly drips from skylights, and multiple glazing reduces the probability of condensation-forming by maintaining an indoor surface temperature much closer to the indoor air temperature.

Heat flow through glazing is due to a combination of conduction, convection and radiation transfers. A few millimetres of glass offers little resistance to heat flow, and most of the thermal resistance due to a single pane of glass is due to surface transfer, being the heat transfer process as convecting air on the warmer side raises the glass surface temperature on that side, and the transfer of heat from the opposite glass surface to the air on the cooler side. Because of the low thermal resistance of the glass, there is little difference between opposite surface temperatures. The effect of each pane in a multiple glazing unit is to add two more surface transfers, thereby reducing the combined conduction and convection effects.

Air is sometimes described as a good insulator, but it has to be stopped from convecting for that to be so. Fibrous insulation materials have this effect, but obviously, such materials cannot be included between the panes of a multiple glazing unit. This space is usually filled with dried air, and inevitably heat transfer by convection occurs. The optimum air gap width is between 12 and 18 mm, as less than 12 mm is insufficient separation, and more than 18 mm permits faster convection currents. A vacuum gap is not practical as the panes would be sucked inwards, but convection can be reduced by replacing the air with a large-molecule inert gas, usually argon. Sealed multiple glazing units are formed by cementing metal or plastic separators around the perimeter of the glazing.

In addition to conduction and convection, heat flow occurs through multiple glazing units by radiant heat transfer between the panes. This can be substantially reduced by panes of low E glass, and it requires a coated surface on just one side of a gap to be effective. As described in the previous chapter, multiple glazing units can be complex. Different types of glazing may be used to provide for light diffusion, solar control, sound insulation or security. Layers of control materials can be added into the gaps, such as

UV blocking plastic film or light-diffusing glass fibre mat. Adjustable light control louvres can be located inside sealed units, with the control motor inside the unit, or with the louvre operated magnetically from outside. Multiple glazing units may be located in the outside skin of the building, or they may be used to separate climatically different zones within a building, such as a gallery and a plenum space.

Electric lighting typologies   6

Many artworks suffered from excessive exposure in the early daylit art galleries, and this brought about a reaction against daylight that was particularly pronounced in the period of reconstruction that followed the Second World War. Electric lighting was seen to be the safe alternative, and new galleries were often designed for little or no daylight, while many existing galleries had their fenestration blanked off. A few electric lighting systems were developed specifically for museum and art gallery use, but for many years they made little headway against the display lighting systems that were widely marketed for commercial display applications. Many examples of unsatisfactory lighting ensued, with lighting that failed to provide adequately for either visual or conservation requirements.

The aesthetics of electric lighting

The outstanding attributes of electric lighting for museums are *precision* and *constancy*. Highlight and shadow patterns can be defined with levels of sharpness that cannot be matched by sunlight, and contrasts of brightness and colour can be presented that either do not occur, or occur only spasmodically, under daylight. Visual effects can be created with exactness: these effects are not subject to seasonal or diurnal variations, but rather can be maintained over time with constancy and reliability. The ways in which the visual attributes of objects may be revealed by lighting that has the appropriate characteristics has been discussed in Chapter 2, and the ability to match lighting precisely to object attributes is a hallmark of a skilful lighting designer.

The elimination of daylight puts the lighting designer in full control. Carefully contrived effects can be set up and locked into place, so that every visitor will be presented with the intended appearance. Modern controls are capable of providing variation over time, but usually this is not wanted in museums. Instead, the usual aim is to achieve exactly the concept envisioned by the designer, and to provide this without variation for the life of the exhibition. It may be added the constancy of electric lighting

Facing page: J. Paul Getty Museum, Los Angeles, California

finds favour with conservators. As exposure is conventionally assessed as being the product of illuminance and time, constant illuminance makes estimation of cumulative exposure straightforward.

Room surface lighting

As will be explained in Chapter 8, there is good reason for giving attention to how a space will be lit before considering lighting for the displayed objects, and so we will start the examination of electric lighting typologies by looking at ways of lighting room surfaces in museums.

The simplest approach to illumination of room surfaces is to suspend diffusing luminaires within the space to distribute light more-or-less evenly onto ceiling, walls and floor surfaces. This approach is unlikely to be successful in a museum, except perhaps in a situation where the luminaires are themselves display objects.

Figure 6.1: *A variety of forms of room surface lighting in a gallery at the Musée d'Orsay, Paris*

A variety of room surface lighting techniques is employed at the Musée d'Orsay. Figures 6.1 and 6.2 show lighting set into the

tops of short walls to illuminate the ceiling and upper walls; lighting set into ceiling beams to illuminate the ceiling; and the same beams used to conceal lighting that washes wall surfaces. The effect is to give a sense of spaciousness to galleries that might otherwise appear enclosing, particularly to visitors entering from the great space of the Central Aisle (Figure 8.51). It is achieved by use of both linear and compact fluorescent lamps, which in every instance are concealed from direct view. Linear fluorescent lamps are used at the Musée l'Orangerie, where they illuminate a translucent ceiling from above (Figure 6.3). In all of these cases, room surfaces are moderately bright and illumination is thoroughly diffused, so that artworks appear sufficiently lit without being given any emphasis.

Figure 6.2: *More room surface lighting techniques at the Musée d'Orsay*

Figure 6.3: *Diffused overall ceiling lighting by linear fluorescent lamps at the Musée l'Orangerie, Puris*

Figure 6.4: *Diffusing ceiling panels arranged in modules at the Manchester City Art Gallery, Manchester, UK*

Figure 6.5: *This ceiling at the Scuola Grande di San Rocco, Venice, is an illuminated work of art, and becomes the source of overall diffused illumination*

Ceiling lighting systems may expand until the luminaires become the ceiling. Figure 6.4 shows suspended glass panels that form a lowered ceiling level, with fluorescent lighting that provides both direct and indirect lighting to the space. The suspensions also provide support for lighting track, to enable spotlighting onto free-standing displays.

There are times when the ceiling is itself a display object, and it can be difficult to provide effective lighting without the luminaires becoming intrusive. Both the ceiling and the floor at the Scuola Grande di San Rocco appear quite magnificent in Figure 6.5, but as we move into the space, the luminaires become obtrusive (Figure 6.6). For the world's most celebrated ceiling, that of the Sistine Chapel, photography is forbidden, but nearby in the Vatican Museums a more tolerant attitude is taken in the Raphael Room. The detail of the upper walls and the vaulted ceiling into which they merge are revealed by diffused lighting from below (Figure 6.7), and the luminaires that provide this distribution of illumination are literally massive. Fabricated in bronze, they stand almost 2 m tall, and although far more massive than those at the Scuola Grande di San Rocco, they seem less obtrusive because people's sole reason for entering this space is to gaze upwards. In this case there is no cornice separating the ceiling from the walls, but where this does occur there is a temptation to use it for mounting the luminaires, thereby leaving the floor clear. This lighting distribution is often much less satisfactory as it tends to

Figure 6.6: *The luminaires at the Scuola Grande di San Rocco distribute light effectively, but are intrusive*

Figure 6.7: *While the luminaires at the Raphael Room, Vatican City, are massive, they effectively reveal the spectacular ceiling and upper walls*

cut the space into upper and lower volumes, and again nearby, an example of this can be seen in the Vatican Library (Figure 6.8).

Wall lighting, or wall-washing as it may be called, is often used for displaying paintings, drawings and tapestries. Lighting for two-dimensional objects where the aim is to illuminate individual art-works is examined on pages 162–170, but here we consider illumination for an entire wall without emphasis to individual objects displayed on the wall. Many luminaire manufacturers offer wall-washing lighting systems, and Figure 6.9 shows a typical

Figure 6.8: *This cornice lighting at the Vatican Library reveals the ceiling without causing any intrusion into the space, but the walls are thrown into dark contrast*

Figure 6.9: *Wall-washing by incandescent PAR lamps in recessed luminaires at the Nationalgalerie, Berlin*

example, in this case using PAR incandescent lamps in fully recessed luminaires. The manufacturer specifies the mounting distance out from the wall according the wall height, and the maximum spacing between luminaires, to ensure an even distribution of wall illuminance. In this case the ceiling receives no direct light and the floor very little, and the light coloured walls play an important role in providing diffusely reflected light throughout the space. The peripheral light distribution draws attention to the walls, which is where the art is displayed, but at the same time, the bright walls raise the viewer's adaptation state. Inevitably, this will have the effect of causing the artworks to appear darker and less colourful.

The linear fluorescent lamp is well suited to providing a uniform wash of wall lighting, but it is not widely used in museums. Figures 6.10 and 6.11 show an installation of louvred fluorescent luminaires which are suspended, enabling both wall-wash and perimeter uplighting distributions. Linear fluorescent lamps also have the advantage that they can provide uniform illuminance over surfaces at relatively close range, and this can enable illumination to be provided by light reflected from surfaces that are appropriately located and angled. Figures 6.12 and 6.13 show two examples of wall-washing achieved in this way. While wall-washing is widely recognized as a way of lighting displays of wall mounted two-dimensional artworks, it can substantially influence the appearance of space, and also the appearance of three-dimensional works for which the walls form the background. Figures 6.14 and 6.15 illustrate this effect.

Figure 6.10: *Wall-washing by suspended fluorescent luminaires at the Sprengel Museum, Hannover, Germany*

Figure 6.11: *The wall-washing luminaires at the Sprengel Museum*

Figure 6.12: *Wall-washing by recessed fluorescent luminaires which illuminate a curved, white reflector, at the Musée d'Orsay, Paris*

Figure 6.13: *Another example of indirect fluorescent lighting to provide wall-washing, at the Picasso Museum, Paris*

Figures 6.14 and 6.15: *These two views show how the appearance of a sculpture is affected by the lighting of the wall against which it is seen, at the National Gallery of Art, East Building, Washington, DC*

There is another strong reason for paying attention to the illumination of room surfaces. All museums are obliged to provide for safe movement, and this means that visitors are able to proceed with confidence at all times. In locations where designers are striving to reduce visitor's visual adaptation levels, this can produce a conflict. In many countries there are safety standards that have to be complied with, and usually these specify a minimum illuminance on the floor which may be in excess of the design illuminance for the display. The key requirements are to indicate the presence of obstructions, and changes of level or direction. Ways of doing this without giving unduly high overall brightness to room surfaces are discussed in Chapter 8.

Lighting three-dimensional objects

The entire scene in Figure 6.16 has been transformed by the beams from three spotlights focused onto the sculpture. This is far more than the sculpture having been made brighter than its background. The effect of the lighting is that sculpture has become Figure, and the surroundings have become Ground. In Chapter 2 we discussed the three lighting patterns that are formed when a three-dimensional object intercepts a flow of light, and two of the patterns are present in this scene. The strongest (or closest) spotlight is directly above the sculpture, and forms a graded shading pattern on the egg-shaped stone, and a sharply defined pattern on the facetted surface of the block that it leans against. The shadow pattern that it casts onto the floor is dense, sharply defined, and

Figure 6.16: *The spotlighting of this sculpture causes it to be perceived as figure and its surround as ground, at the Queensland Art Gallery, Brisbane, Australia*

small in extent. The other two spotlights, one of which is visible on the facing wall, cast sharp and more extensive shadow patterns, but they are weakened by the overhead spotlight. Although the lighting has sharpness, there is no highlight pattern, or perhaps only a very weak one, due to the smooth but matt stone surfaces. If the surface of the egg-shaped stone was polished, we would see three sharply defined highlights from which we would be able to infer the locations of the spotlights. This ability not merely to draw attention to a three-dimensional object, but to be able to influence its appearance and to interact with its physical attributes, is the facility that spotlighting offers. In the following chapter we will examine the various means by which this type of lighting may be controlled, but in this chapter we look at the range of interactions of directed light and objects that may be achieved, and how they may affect object appearance.

Before launching into the more creative applications of spotlighting, we should not overlook that it is often used to overcome lighting conflicts, particularly those due to side windows. Figure 6.17 shows a perimeter of floor-to-ceiling glass combined with a dark ceiling and floor. This is a situation that could not be overcome by diffused illumination, and strong spotlighting is needed. It can be seen that several of the objects on display are very dark in

Figure 6.17: *The bright perimeter of this gallery space requires strong spotlighting to achieve competing brightness, at the Nationalgalerie, Berlin*

Figure 6.18: *Without the spotlighting, these sculptures at the Metropolitan Museum of Art, New York, would be seen in silhouette*

colour, requiring pools of light to be focused onto the light-coloured surfaces against which they are seen. Figure 6.18 shows another example where, from this viewpoint, the sculpture would be seen in silhouette. The film used has somewhat exaggerated the colour difference of the daylight and the spotlighting, but this makes it easy to see how the shading pattern has been influenced by the spotlighting. A rather more subtle effect is shown in Figure 6.19. A pleasant balance of spotlighting with bright window has been achieved, and while the flow of light is inconsistent with the obvious source of light, the result is an attractive shading pattern on the sculpture.

Figure 6.19: *The appearance of this sculpture viewed against a window gains form gentle spotlighting at the Clark Institute, Williamstown, Massachusetts*

Figure 6.20: *The appearance of this sculpture is influenced by the combined effects of its architectural setting and the spotlighting. National Gallery of Art, West Building, Washington, DC*

Spotlighting may be used to draw attention, and where this clearly is consistent with the architectural design, the result can be quite dramatic (Figure 6.20). Such emphasis cannot be achieved where several objects compete for attention, but similar lighting may be effectively used to reveal form, texture and detail with high levels of clarity (Figure 6.21). Where the same lighting approach is extended to a group of objects, these goals may still be achievable, but one is likely to be more conscious of the artificial nature of the setting, particularly where the ambient illumination is low. Perhaps an unnatural appearance was a design intent in Figure 6.22, for nearby in the same institution an altogether different lighting effect is provided for a group of sculptures where spotlighting is combined with a higher ambient illumination (Figure 6.23).

Sculpture lends itself to spotlighting, both because of the lighting patterns that can be generated, and because most sculpture is,

Figure 6.21: *Form, texture and detail are revealed by individually spotlighting objects at the Simon Norton Art Gallery, Pasadena, California*

Figure 6.22: *The effect of individual spotlighting with low ambient illumination at the Metropolitan Museum of Art, New York*

thankfully, non-responsive to light exposure. In Figure 6.24, the sculpture has thoughtfully been juxtaposed with a two-dimensional work of similar artistic intent, and it is evident that the lighting designer has used spotlighting to good effect. In this case, the visible effect is a shading pattern which benefits from a lack of sharpness in the lighting. In Figure 6.25, the surface quality of Degas' *Little dancer aged 14 years* is revealed by the highlight pattern, which depends on lighting having sharpness. The remarkable glowing form of the sculpture in Figure 6.26 is due both to the sharpness of the spotlighting, and to the fact that it stands in a daylit space and this photograph was taken late on a winter afternoon.

On a trip to the National Gallery of Scotland, lighting designer Kevan Shaw showed me some remarkable examples of spotlighting. The ancient stones shown in Figure 6.27 had been in the museum's collection for many years, but had attracted little attention. It wasn't until Kevan lit them that visitors became aware of

Figure 6.23: *Individual spotlighting with higher ambient illumination, and a more consistent 'flow of light', also at the Metropolitan Museum of Art*

Figure 6.25: *Degas' sculpture stands in a daylit space, and gains from 'sharpness' due to spotlighting. The Clark Institute, Williamstown, Massachusetts*

Figure 6.24: *The display of this non-responsive sculpture gains both from emphasis by spotlighting, and being juxtaposed with a painting of similar subject. The Clark Institute, Williamstown, Massachusetts*

Figure 6.26: *This scene shows a daylit space at the Metropolitan Museum of Art, late on a winter afternoon when the ambient illumination has faded and the supplementary lighting dominates to give striking visual effects*

Figure 6.27: *These ancient stone tablets at the National Museum of Scotland, Edinburgh, had attracted little attention until this shadow pattern was revealed by spotlighting (with permission, Kevan Shaw)*

Figure 6.28: *Spotlighting used to frame a view, at the National Museum of Scotland (with permission, Kevan Shaw)*

the images that they held. At another point Kevan showed how he had lit both a display and framed it with its background (Figure 6.28), and how he had used shadow to tell a tale. In Figure 6.29, the object visible through the archway is a portable guillotine, which was employed for many years by a travelling Scottish court. As visitors approach the archway, the guillotine is revealed in stark silhouette, and the shadow reaches across to touch the tomb in the foreground.

Some three-dimensional objects depend on sharpness to form crisp shadow and highlight patterns, and the Rodin sculpture in Figure 6.30 is such an object. The lighting reveals not only the contrasts of gloss and texture of the metal surfaces, but also the colours of the different metals used which, as explained in Chapter 2, are revealed by specular reflections rather than diffuse reflections, as is the case for pigments. Spotlighting also has facility to reveal the body colours of glass and other transparent materials,

Figure 6.29: *Use of shadow to connect displayed objects, at the National Museum of Scotland (with permission, Kevan Shaw)*

Figure 6.30: *The highlight pattern on this sculpture reveals not only surface texture, but also the contrasting colours of the different metals, at the Rodin Museum, Philadelphia, Pennsylvania. This effect depends on lighting that has 'sharpness'*

Figure 6.31: *It is again a highlight pattern that reveals the brilliant colours of this glass mosaic decorated column at the Metropolitan Museum of Art, New York*

as seen in the lighting of an architectural column decorated with glass mosaic from Louis Comfort Tiffany's home (Figure 6.31). Glass can be a difficult material to display, depending on the attributes that are to be revealed. Some are best revealed by transmission and some by surface reflection, and this can create conflicts. However, when surface reflection is what is needed, spotlighting has the answer. The display of a glass sculpture at the Corning Glass Museum (Figure 6.32) shows spotlighting being used to great effect.

Shadow patterns may also play a part in display. The sculpture shown in Figure 6.33 gains apparent solidity and separation from the wall due to the double shadow pattern cast onto the wall.

Figure 6.32: *A clear glass sculpture revealed by reflected and refracted highlight patterns at the Corning Glass Museum, Corning, New York*

Figure 6.33: *The shadow pattern due to the spotlighting gives this object solidity and separation from the wall. Simon Norton Art Gallery, Pasadena, California*

Lighting designer Gordon Anson at National Art Gallery, Washington, DC, believes that the cast shadow should be seen as an intrinsic part of the display, and he has demonstrated this dramatically in his presentations of sculpture (Figures 6.34, 6.35).

Figure 6.34: *Spotlighting used to reveal form both by shading patterns on the sculptures, and by shadow patterns on surrounding surfaces. National Gallery of Art, West Building, Washington, DC*

Figure 6.35: *Another striking example of shadow patterns at the National Gallery of Art*

Figure 6.36: *A remarkable halo effect created by spotlighting at the Denver Art Museum, Denver, Colorado*

Sometime serendipity plays a part. Exhibition designer Jeremy Hillhouse at the Denver Art Museum was directing a spotlight onto an altarpiece when a halo appeared (Figure 6.36). He liked it, and he locked the spotlight in that position. By doing this, he was able to secure an ephemeral condition for all to see.

Lighting two-dimensional objects

While we think of all manner of pictures as being two-dimensional objects, this is not strictly accurate. When artists apply paint thickly, perhaps trowelling the paint or applying an impasto technique, they are raising the surface into the third dimension. These surfaces generate light and shade patterns in an oblique 'flow of light', as will collage and fabric art. Another dimension is added when artists employ glazes to affect the scattering of incident light, and as discussed in Chapter 2, the concept of the 'sharpness' of lighting may be invoked to describe the propensity of lighting to form reflected highlights. Even when we do have a flat and totally matt surface, as may occur for a watercolour or pastel drawing, we can expect that the artwork will be displayed behind glass, and so it has to be seen through the image formed by a weak mirror. Lighting two-dimensional objects usually involves three-dimensional factors.

Figure 6.37 shows the formation of the reflected image of a light source in a vertical picture plane, where the image of the source is as far behind the reflection plane as the source is in front of it, and the line connecting the image and source intersects the plane at right angles. For viewer 1 the image occurs above the picture, and unless the art gallery has unwisely opted for glossy wall finishes, no reflected image of the luminaire will be apparent within this viewer's field of view. Viewer 2 is shorter, or might be a wheelchair user, or advances closer, and sees the image reflected in the upper part of the picture. If the picture is glazed, a sharply formed image will be apparent that may be quite distracting. Whether or not the picture is glazed, reflection at the picture surface will form a spread area of specularly reflected brightness that will be apparent to the second viewer, and in this zone colours will appear desaturated and detail will be partially or totally obscured. The extent of this effect will depend on both the luminaire and the surface reflection properties of the picture, but it can be avoided by tilting the picture forwards, as shown in Figure 6.38. The location of the potentially detrimental image may be plotted by projecting the picture plane to include the intersection point of the connecting line. Nothing else has changed from Figure 6.37, but now neither viewer will see a light source image superimposed on the picture. The downside of this change is that the incidence of light onto the picture has become more oblique, and if the light source is relocated to overcome this, the reflected image in the top of the picture is likely to return.

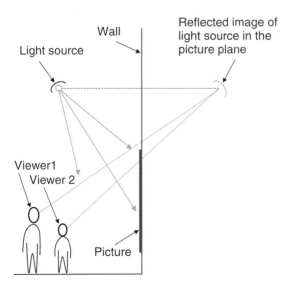

Figure 6.37: *Reflected image of a luminaire for a vertical picture plane. For viewer 2, veiling reflections will occur where the image coincides with the picture*

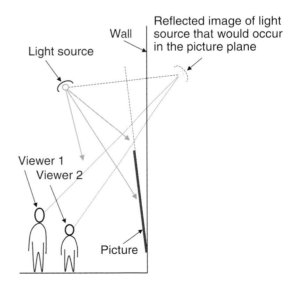

Figure 6.38: *Reflected image of a luminaire for a tilted picture plane. Neither viewer will experience veiling reflections, but the wall surface must be matt to ensure avoidance of reflected glare*

There are some helpful 'rules of thumb' for locating luminaires in a picture gallery, but as there are always exceptions to rules, it is necessary to understand what they are based on. With regard to vertical picture planes, the critical factors are:

• How far up the wall does the picture hanging area extend?

• How much height is available for mounting the luminaires?

• What is the lowest viewer's eye level that has to be allowed for?

• How close to the picture may this viewer approach before luminaire images become visible?

It is a matter of common observation that people tend to stand back from a large painting, and will approach closely to a miniature painting. A useful planning guide is known as the '40 degrees rule', but somewhat guardedly I wish to make it clear that I know of absolutely no research basis for this 'rule'. However, the claim is that people will naturally tend to adjust their viewing distance from an image so that its width or height, whichever is the greater, subtends an angle of approximately 40° at the eye. If I hand you a postage stamp, a postcard, or a wall calendar, the suggestion is that you will hold each image in front of you at such a distance that it forms an angle of 40° at your eye. By way of support, it may be noted that an image taken with a 35 mm camera fitted with a 50 mm focal length lens 'looks right', in that a shorter focal length gives a 'wide angle' view and a longer focal length gives a 'telephoto' effect. A lens of 50 mm focal length focussed onto the 36 mm wide image format gives a viewing angle of 40°. So keeping an open mind, we can examine how this 'rule' may be applied.

It is not unknown for museum directors to insist that pictures be hung on any part of a hanging wall surface, but that is an impossible demand. It is also impossible to demand that viewers should be able to approach right up to large paintings without seeing luminaire images at any part of the surface. The principal angles governing the viewing of vertically mounted paintings or other two-dimensional artworks are shown in Figure 6.39. The viewer has positioned himself, or herself, for a 40° vertical viewing angle of the picture hanging area, and for this type of situation, his distance from the wall will be approximately 1.4 times the height of the hanging area. This assumes that the picture he is looking at is in 'portrait format', but if it is a large work in 'landscape format', he will stand further back to achieve the 40° viewing angle, so reflection-free viewing will be achieved with a greater margin. If he decides to approach closer to examine a small picture, all will continue to be well providing the picture is located at around his

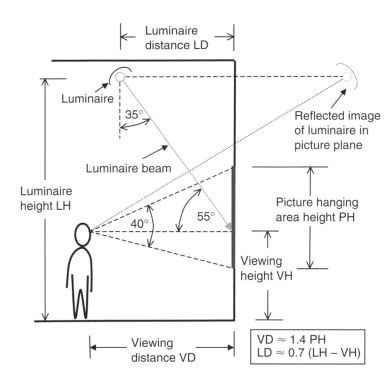

Figure 6.39: *Some interrelationships of angles and dimensions for lighting two-dimensional works*

eye level. The image of the luminaire will coincide with the hanging area above the top of the picture, and it will not be visible if the hanging area has a sufficiently matt surface.

The next factor to consider is the luminaire location. Height is an advantage, and usually luminaires will be mounted close to or recessed into the ceiling. Another handy rule of thumb is to locate the luminaires so that the distance from the wall is 0.7 times the luminaire height from the wall minus the viewing height, for which a typical viewer eye level is often assumed to be 1.5 metres above floor level. Two justifications for this rule may be advanced. One is that this arrangement forms an incidence angle of 55° at eye level (note that the incidence angle is measured relative to the normal, not to the wall), and experience has shown this to work well. A higher incidence angle causes excessive light and shade patterns on rough-textured works, and frame shadows may obscure too much of the upper part of a picture. Conversely, a lesser incidence angle produces a rather flat lighting effect, as well as making reflected luminaire images difficult to avoid. The second justification is to consider how would the illuminance at the point shown in the figure where the luminaire beam strikes the picture plane be affected by increasing or reducing the luminaire distance from the wall? Any reader familiar with the inverse square and cosine laws of illumination can confirm for themselves that for a spotlight luminaire, the maximum value is achieved when the incidence angle equals 55°.

Wall-washing is a lighting technique that achieves a uniform illuminance over a wall surface by use of luminaires designed to give a light distribution suited to this purpose, and the characteristics of this light distribution are discussed in the following chapter. Wall-washing may be applied not only to walls, but also to free-standing screens and other displays of two-dimensional artworks (Figure 6.40), although care has to be taken to avoid glare to viewers on the opposite side of the screen. This type of lighting gives no emphasis to any of the displayed objects. Alternatively each artwork may be illuminated by a separate spotlight, so that the scallop patterns on the wall mark out individual territories (Figure 6.41). For a less pronounced effect, diffusing filters can be added to the spotlights to soften the beam edges and merge the separate pools of light (Figure 6.42).

The ultimate of individual lighting control is provided by the 'beam-shaper' or framing spotlight. This luminaire has an optical system similar to that of a slide projector, so that a hard-edged beam can be precisely focused onto a surface. The beam can be shaped by manipulating shutters on the luminaire, so that the beam can be exactly fitted to the rectangular perimeter of an artwork. The visual effect can be heightened by concealing the luminaire, which is usually done by mounting it above the ceiling and lighting the artwork through a small aperture in the ceiling. Some restraint should be applied in using this technique, because if carried to excess an unnatural appearance can occur. A painting may lose the appearance of paint on canvas and instead look more like a trans-illuminated transparency, and this is particularly likely to

Figure 6.40: *Spotlighting for display of two-dimensional works on screens in a large space with high ceiling, and relatively high ambient illumination. Queensland Art Gallery, Brisbane, Australia*

Figure 6.41: *Spotlighting for display of two-dimensional works with relatively low ambient illumination, so that each artwork has its own territory defined by a scallop of light. National Gallery of Victoria, Melbourne, Australia*

Figure 6.42: *Spotlighting two-dimensional artworks in low ambient illumination with merged, soft-edge beams. The Getty Center, Santa Monica, California*

occur in situations where the ambient illumination is low. Figure 6.43 shows a framing spotlight illuminating a large artwork, and Figure 6.44 shows a row of small artworks, each with its own tailored beam of light. This type of lighting tends to emphasize the colourfulness of the artworks. An alternative way of achieving that objective, albeit with a very different overall visual effect, is to employ conventional lighting but to surround the artworks with low reflectance surfaces, as shown in Figure 6.45.

A traditional approach to lighting individual paintings has been a picture light, comprising a tubular incandescent lamp in a metal reflector, supported by a metal arm projecting from a mounting point on the wall above the top of the picture. Far too often the visual effect has been disastrous. The top of the picture is overlit and the bottom is underlit, with this unwanted gradient being given emphasis by the specular reflection of the lamp in the top of the picture. For lighting the Frick Collection, William Allen designed picture lights to suit each of the two-dimensional artworks. They are quite difficult to see in Figures 6.46 and 6.47 as they are

Figure 6.43: *Spotlighting a two-dimensional artwork with a recessed framing spotlight. Calouste Gulbenkian Museum, Lisbon*

Figure 6.44: *A series of small two-dimensional works, each illuminated by its own framing spotlight. Calouste Gulbenkian Museum*

Figure 6.45: *The combination of low ambient illumination and framing spotlights give these artworks enhanced brightness and colourfulness. Musée de Beaux Arts, Lille, France*

Figure 6.46: *With relatively high ambient daylight illumination, this redesign of the traditional picture lighting luminaire provides for visibility of the pictures without a noticeably enhanced effect. The Frick Collection, New York*

Figure 6.47: *In a room adjacent to where the previous figure was photographed, the effect to the picture lighting becomes more noticeable with lower ambient illumination. The Frick Collection, New York*

Figure 6.48: *The scene in this picture is lit from below, and so the museum has provided lighting from below. Isobella Stewart Gardner Museum, Boston, Massachusetts*

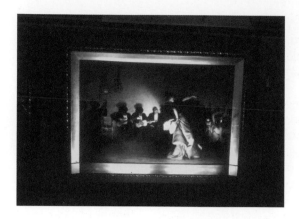

painted to match the walls, but in appearance they are quite similar to the traditional units. They have been carefully located to avoid veiling reflections, and they differ in that they house 25 mm diameter tungsten halogen reflector lamps, with the wattages and beam angles chosen to enable them to be aimed to provide an even distribution of illuminance over the whole surface of each picture. In some cases, additional lamps are used to spotlight objects displayed on furniture below the pictures.

Locating luminaires to avoid veiling reflections in glass is explained in the following section, and the principles apply equally to pictures, even if they are unglazed. Although the clearly defined reflection of a luminaire due to glazing appears more intrusive than the more diffused highlight reflected from the surface of an unglazed oil painting, the highlight is still diluting colour and concealing detail. Usually picture lighting is provided from above, but occasionally there are departures from this rule. At the Isobella Stewart Gardner Museum, a painting is lit from below to match the flow of light that is depicted in the scene (Figure 6.48).

Case lighting

The need to protect museum objects with a layer of glass or clear plastic is an unfortunate intrusion into display, but it is unavoidable and both exhibitions designers and lighting designers simply have to come to terms with this fact. In the previous section we examined how to locate the reflected image of a luminaire due to the glazing of a framed picture. The essential difference when we consider case lighting is that the displayed object is set back some distance behind the glass, and this opens up two opportunities which avoid the luminaire reflection problems associated with picture lighting. We can light the case internally, or we can light it externally through a glazed top surface. However, before we examine examples of case lighting, we will look more carefully at reflections caused by glazing materials.

Figure 6.49 shows a ray of unpolarized light incident on a pane of glazing material, which may be glass or a clear plastic, such as acrylic or polycarbonate. Reflection at the first surface that the ray encounters depends on the angle of incidence i, and the refractive index of the glazing. Refractive index values for soda-lime (common) glass and clear plastics are similar (approximately $\mu = 1.5$) and for incidence angles up to 45°, reflectance will be approximately 4 per cent. This increases gradually to 10 per cent at 60°, and then rapidly increases to total reflection as the incidence angle approaches 90°. It can also be seen in the figure that while the bulk of the incident ray is transmitted through the glazing, with the principal emergent ray being parallel to the incident ray but with some displacement, multiple reflections and emergent rays also occur which can have the effect of doubling the total reflected light to approximately 8 per cent. It may be noted that this added contribution to reflection is greatest when the total of absorbed light within the body of the glazing is very low.

Generally the clear plastics used for museum cases are 'water clear', but this may not be so for glass. The characteristics of common soda-lime glass that is widely used for window glazing have been discussed in Chapter 5, where it was noted that the slight green tint in this type of glass is due to iron impurities in the basic

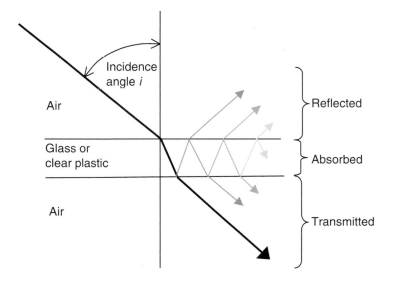

Figure 6.49: *Incident ray, and its reflected, absorbed and transmitted components*

ingredients from which glass is manufactured. This tint is clearly visible if a pane of glass is viewed edge on, and can be quite noticeable when viewing through panes that are 12 mm thick or more. Low-iron glass is available, but it is considerably more expensive than soda-lime glass. While the increased cost may be considered unjustifiable for windows, it might be found acceptable for cases. There are several reasons why this can be so. Slightly tinted window glazing will affect all the daylight entering a space, and viewers will adapt to the ambient illumination and this will govern their assessment of coloured materials. When they encounter a display case, the view through case glazing will be assessed relative to their state of visual adaptation, and this may cause even a slight tint to appear noticeable. In the case of an externally illuminated case, such as a clear-top case, the light reaching the viewer has undergone two transmissions through the glazing. Also, it may be necessary to use thick glass, perhaps because the pane size is large or to provide security, which increases the visual effect of the iron content. Finally, the total area of case glazing is likely to be small in relation to the sum of window area.

Ideally, the glazing would absorb none of the light, and in this case we could assume that for incidence angles of not more than 45°, we will have 92 per cent light transmission and 8 per cent reflection. While there are no glazing materials that actually achieve this, there are both plastics and glasses which, for normal glazing thicknesses, come very close. This means that the best we can hope for is that a viewer will see 92 per cent of the luminance of the displayed object, while superimposed over this view will be an 8 per cent reflected image of themselves and whatever is beside or behind them. If the ambient illumination is low relative to that of the displayed object, and if there are no displays behind the viewer, this condition may appear quite satisfactory. However, it often will happen that the viewer is surrounded by other brightly lit displays, and this causes us to take a look at anti-reflection coatings.

Anti-reflection coating (sometimes referred to as non-reflecting glass) is achieved by a thin transparent film applied to the glass surface. In the field of optics, thin-film technology may involve multiple layers to provide specialized properties, but for panes of glass the most common form of anti-reflection coating comprises a single layer of magnesium fluoride (MgF_2). Figure 6.50 shows a much enlarged section through such a coating. Reflection and refraction occur where the incident ray meets the coating surface, but because the refractive index of magnesium fluoride is intermediate between those of air and glass ($\mu = 1.38$), both of these effects are less than would occur at an air/glass interface. The transmitted ray arrives at the coating/glass interface, and again, reduced levels of reflection and refraction occur. A second reflected ray emerges from the coating parallel to the initial reflected ray, and because it has undergone the double path through the coating, it is delayed in time. Assume that the incident ray is monochromatic (i.e. light of one specific wavelength) and from the middle of the visible spectrum, that is to say, it has a wavelength of 550 nanometres and it would appear to us to have a saturated yellowish-green colour. To the right of Figure 6.50 we see the waveforms of both reflected rays, and the result of the delay is that the two waveforms are half a phase out of synchronization, so that their sum equals zero. This form of cancellation is termed destructive interference, and while the wavelength at which it achieves maximum effect is affected by the angle of incidence, it is principally determined by the coating thickness. A thickness of one quarter of the wavelength of the incident light ($\lambda/4$) is optimum, so to minimize visible reflections, the coating thickness has to be 550/4 = 137.5 nanometres. Bearing in mind that a nanometre is a millionth of a millimetre, it can be seen that the manufacture of this type of glass in large panes calls for very precise quality control. It will also be apparent that such glass cannot be optimally effective at all visible wavelengths, and so while the overall effect will be to substantially reduce the reflected component, such reflected images as do occur will comprise light from both ends of the visible spectrum. In many cases these images will be too dim to be noticeable, but they may be visible where there is a combination of brightly displayed objects and low ambient illumination. Figure 6.51 shows such an example, and while the visibility of the displayed object is excellent, it appears surrounded by ghostly magenta-coloured images of itself.

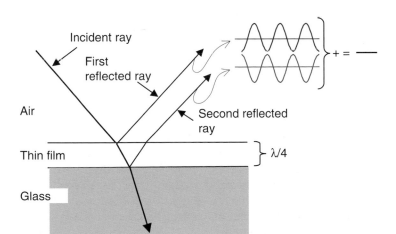

Figure 6.50: *Destructive interference due to an anti-reflection coating. When the two reflected rays are 180° out of phase, their sum is zero. While maximum interference depends on the incidence angle, the optimum film thickness is around one quarter wavelength ($\lambda/4$) of the incident ray*

Figure 6.51: *The anti-reflection case glazing provides well for the visibility of this display, but it also provides dim, magenta-tinted reflections in the distance. Rijksmuseum, Shipol Airport, Amsterdam*

There are several forms of protection that cases and their glazing may be required to provide. Security may be concerned with theft or vandalism, and may even require bullet-proof glazing. These materials comprise multiple laminates of glass and plastic interlayers, where reflections at interfaces are avoided by ensuring that all the materials are matched for refractive index. Glazing may be required to protect objects from ultraviolet exposure, and acrylic plastics and laminated glass (see Chapter 5) with various levels of UV blocking performance are available. These forms of protection may be required in older daylit sculpture galleries that lack UV-blocking glazing, and may be employed as useful insurance against maintenance staff failing to replace UV filters after servicing luminaires, or for filters failing to maintain their performance over time. Sealed cases may be used to maintain the displayed objects in a controlled environment, such as a low-oxygen atmosphere, to reduce rates of chemical change. All these factors affect choices of glazing materials and how they are to be installed.

The great majority of cases provide for viewing through vertical glazing, with either internal lighting or lighting through a glazed top surface. While these characteristics are common, other aspects of case design show countless variations. Cases may provide for viewing from one side, more than one side, or from all around. They may be divided into layers by solid shelves, and internal lighting can take many forms. Designers must never overlook the importance of surface reflectance values, and for lighting that is from above or from below, vertical glazing becomes an effective reflector. This reflection from the inside glazing surfaces can provide a useful means of getting light onto the vertical faces of displayed objects, and it needs to be noted that when checking illuminance values of displayed objects for compliance with conservation standards, readings need to be taken with case doors closed.

The range of sizes of the objects to be displayed is a major factor in case design. Figure 6.52 shows an example of a combination of wall inset cases and clear-top cases to enable small objects to be examined at close range. All of the lighting is tungsten halogen spotlights, and it can be seen that the inset cases receive light from built-in lighting above the cases and also from ceiling-mounted spotlights, which light the forward edges of the cases bases strongly, providing upward reflection onto the display objects. It should be noted that lighting cases externally may produce noticeable patterns of reflected light onto other surfaces. Other examples of case lighting, also at the Arthur M. Sackler Gallery of the Smithsonian Institution, show clear-top cases used to draw attention to a particular object in a grouped display (Figure 6.53), and enabling all-round viewing of three-dimensional objects (Figure 6.54). These views show effects of surface reflectance values. In the first case, the wall-mounted displays appear to glow against their dark background, despite the fact that the wall-wash lighting provides a uniform illuminance. The selected display in the free-standing case is also seen against dark-coloured background surfaces, and although I was not able to check the illuminance values, I formed the opinion that they were not more than 50 lux. The urns displayed in the second

Figure 6.52: *A combination of wall-inset and clear-top cases to present objects of differing sizes at the Arthur M. Sackler Gallery, Smithsonian Institution, Washington, DC*

Figure 6.53: *A group of two-dimensional objects is given focus by featuring one for three-dimensional display and all-round viewing in a clear-top case, at the Arthur M. Sackler Gallery*

Figure 6.54: *Three-dimensional objects presented for all-round viewing, with external case lighting. The Arthur M. Sackler Gallery*

view are certainly lit to a higher level, and in this case, light-coloured surfaces are used below the objects to soften the flow of light and improve visibility of the shadowed surfaces.

Lectern cases, as shown in Figures 8.33 and 8.34, have been popular for displaying documents and other works on paper, but are not often seen these days. For their display of Old Masters Drawings, the Getty Center employs display cases with vertical glazing and a display surface tilted back 20° (see Figures 8.44–8.46). This surface is lit from above to 50 lux by a fibre-optics system with a tungsten halogen illuminator, and the arrangement allows viewers the choice of standing back or approaching close, without putting security at risk or casting shadows over the display. For those cases that do not face another case, the viewing conditions are very satisfactory.

Where a case is designed for a specific object, there is the opportunity to also design the lighting to suit the specific features of the object. Both the form and the rich metallic colours of the urn in Figure 6.55 are revealed by the diffused lighting from below, while the ornate handles are picked out by spotlights from above. The stunning appearance of the bowl shown in Figure 6.56 is achieved by intense light entering the diffusing glass through a small aperture in the mirror on which it stands.

A time-honoured way of lighting cases is by means of a 'light attic', this being a box-like enclosure that forms the top of the case, and houses the lamps that illuminate the case interior, usually through some form of translucent material. Fluorescent lamps mounted above white plastic 'egg-crate' louvre had long been popular before low-brightness parabolic-cell louvre largely replaced the white plastic. More recently there has been a tendency towards spotlight sources, usually tungsten halogen but sometimes low-wattage metal halide, to gain the advantages of lighting that can be directed onto specific objects, and which can give 'sharpness' to the lighting in the forms of reflected and refracted highlights and sharply defined shadow patterns. Figure 6.57 shows an example of such lighting where objects that are non-responsive to light exposure permit high display illuminance values, and such displays are able to compete with the brightness of adjacent daylight, as shown in Figure 6.58. The need to limit exposure for light-responsive objects does not eliminate opportunities for eye-catching displays, as the solution lies in restricting the ambient illumination. Figure 6.59 shows historic North American Indian feather headdresses displayed at restricted illuminance values in a light-attic case, where the display lighting is the only source of illumination and views to adjoining spaces have been avoided. The full-height glazing has virtually disappeared.

Figure 6.55: *Internal case lighting from below gives good visibility over the whole surface of this object. Shanghai Museum, Shanghai*

Figure 6.56: *This artwork is illuminated through a hole in the mirror base, so that light is diffused into glass and causes it to glow. Corning Museum of Glass, Corning, New York*

The use of fibre optics systems has enabled all-glass cases without light-attics or other devices for concealing the luminaires, as shown in Figure 6.60. Each fibre terminal is fitted with a lens for beam control, and can be directionally adjusted. In this case the lighting from below is from fluorescent lamps, but fibre outlets can be located in the base of the case, under shelves, or within the supporting framework. Close-range lighting applications are discussed in Chapter 7, pps 204–206.

Figure 6.57: *The light attic is an effective way of providing internal case illumination and minimizing risks of reflected glare. Queensland Museum of Art, Brisbane, Australia*

Figure 6.58: *In the vicinity of views to the outdoors, objects in display cases need to be restricted to non-responsive materials so that light levels can compete with daylight. Queensland Museum of Art*

In some instances, the cases actually form the museum interior. Figure 6.61 shows a display case which, with its lighting attic, divides a space into separate galleries while nonetheless permitting a view through. The displayed objects, some supported on a glass shelf, form the division of this space. Perhaps more significantly, cases can become the surrounding walls of the gallery. Figure 6.62 shows artworks at the Hong Kong Art Gallery which never were intended to be seen in frames. Fluorescent wall-washing inside the cases provides even illumination of the wall surfaces, without emphasis to any of the works. In this way, the viewer is surrounded by walls hung with art and is barely conscious of the presence of cases.

Figure 6.59: *The glazing of this light attic case virtually disappears, as it is in a very low ambient illumination setting. National Museum of Art, East Building, Washington, DC*

Figure 6.60: *Fibre optics distribute light to a multiplicity of outlets, each of which may be adjustable for direction and focus. Manchester City Art Gallery, Manchester, UK*

Supplementing daylight

It is not unusual for daylit galleries to require some electric lighting during daylight hours, perhaps to overcome gloom in parts remote from the fenestration or to give emphasis to selected displays. All daylit galleries require electric lighting for night-time use, and inevitably there will be transitional periods during which the electric lighting is used in conjunction with fading daylight. All of these conditions require careful thought. It has been a theme of this chapter that these two forms of lighting have their own aesthetics, and this creates conflicts when they are used together. I comment in passing that I dislike the distinction of 'natural' and 'artificial' lighting because the word artificial has connotations of inferiority. Electric lighting can achieve visual effects that are not attainable by daylight, and designers should turn their minds towards exploiting the potential that electric lighting offers rather than starting with the mindset that it is a substitute for daylight.

The most obvious problem encountered in supplementing daylight with electric lighting is the difference in colour appearance. It is a matter of common experience that when we are fully adapted to daylight, the common forms of electric lighting may appear to give a yellowish cast to whatever they are illuminating, but if we return at night time when the whole space is lit by electric lighting, the same lighting appears acceptably white. However, when we examine how lighting affects the appearance of specific objects, more factors come into play.

I visited the Musée de Louvre on a bright sunny day in March 1997, and one of my target destinations was the Venus de Milo. Following the museum guide, I rounded a corner and in the distance I caught my first view of the Venus, framed by arches, flooded with daylight, and surrounded by people (Figure 6.63). I worked my way through the crowd and eventually gained a vantage point (Figure 6.64). She is beautiful, and of course my preconditioned eye caused me to admire the interaction of her form with the flow of light. The shading patterns softly moulded her rounded contours, and in the absence of sharpness, the shadows cast by her nose, chin and breasts merged with the shading patterns. There was no sunlight entering the gallery, so that the source of light was the patch of sky visible through a window only a short distance away. This large, diffuse source provided the lateral illumination vector, and as the surrounding surfaces were mostly of quite low reflectance, the vector/scalar ratio would have been fairly high and the 'flow of light' appeared moderately strong. I found the overall effect to be very satisfactory.

Figure 6.61: *This display case with built-in lighting subdivides the space to form separate galleries, while providing viewing of the objects from both sides, as well as views between the galleries. Museum fur Kunsthandwerk, Frankfurt, Germany*

Figure 6.62: *These wall hangings were not meant to be seen in display cases, so the walls have become cases and are washed with light from fluorescent luminaires. Hong Kong Art Gallery, Hong Kong*

Figure 6.63: *The Venus de Milo is instantly recognizable at a distance, and draws the visitors. The Louvre, Paris*

Figure 6.64: *The Venus de Milo at the Louvre in a 'flow of light' due to diffused daylight that generates moderately strong shading patterns, which are slightly counteracted by electric lighting*

I returned to the Venus late on a November afternoon in 2005. The daylight had almost completely faded, and since my previous visit new electric lighting had been installed. The interaction of form and light was quite different (Figure 6.65). Spotlights mounted above and to both sides produce a downward vector direction, causing shading of the eyes affecting the appearance of her face. The spotlights cause sharp-edged shadows below the chin, and while there is cast shadow beneath the breasts, the torso lacks the modelling that was previously evident. I returned the following morning when the weather was bright and sunny, and this time the Venus was lit by a combination of daylight and electric lighting (Figure 6.66). The daylight was dominant on her face, and here the earlier appearance was largely restored, but the body lacked the dynamic appearance that had been given

Figure 6.65: *The Venus de Milo on a late afternoon, when daylight has faded. The electric lighting has been increased since the previous view, but at this time the appearance would be dominated by the electric lighting*

Figure 6.66: *The Venus de Milo on a bright morning. The daylight probably is similar to Figure 6.64, but the stronger electric lighting has the effect of weakening the 'flow of light' and the shading patterns it generates*

by the lateral flow of light on my first visit. Undoubtedly the surface of the Venus is made more visible by addition of the electric lighting, but the reduction of shading patterns and the lack of a distinct 'flow of light' left me with a feeling of disappointment.

I do not presume that all readers will see these lighting effects in the same way as I do, but I do believe that everyone involved in providing lighting for daylit galleries should be aware that changes of appearance will inevitably occur when daylight changes from the dominant to the lesser source.

Self-luminous art objects

Thus far the purpose of electric lighting has been to provide the illumination that reveals museum exhibits, but not all of these objects need illumination. As an unusual example, the Picasso Museum contains a luminaire designed by the artist (Figure 6.67).

Self-luminous artworks may range from quite compact works, such as the decorative shadow patterns shown in Figure 6.68, to sprawling works that extend through a substantial gallery area, such as the composition of fluorescent lamps and glossy black corrugated steel shown in Figure 6.69. For such works, designers have the difficult task of providing effective blackout while ensuring that visitors are provided with sufficient illumination to ensure their safety.

A growing category of museum exhibits is projected images, and here again they can take many forms. The Urbis Museum provides viewing stations to enable visitors to interact with a variety of images and informational material (Figures 6.70 to 6.72), and the brightness of these images is sufficient not to require blackout conditions. At the Hong Kong Art Gallery, projected art takes its place in a gallery alongside more conventional art (Figure 6.73).

Figure 6.67: *A gallery lit by a luminaire designed by the artist. The Picasso Museum, Paris*

Figure 6.68: *It is the lighting that creates the art. Museum of Modern Art, New York*

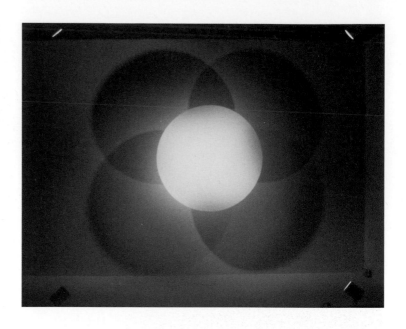

Figure 6.69: *Self-luminous art that needs no ambient or display lighting. Artist: Ralph Hotere. Te Papa/ National Museum of New Zealand, Wellington*

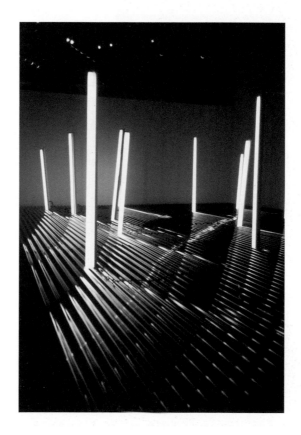

Figure 6.70: *Projected displays at Urbis, Manchester, UK*

Figure 6.71: *Separate display panels at Urbis to enable interaction with viewers*

Figure 6.72: *Visitors are exposed to a succession of projection display panels at Urbis*

Figure 6.73: *Visitors pause for a projected art display that is presented among other wall-mounted artworks, at the Hong Kong Museum of Art, Hong Kong*

Electric lighting controls 7

The controllability of electric lighting is its great asset. For a designer who has in mind a particular appearance for a display, or for a complete exhibition, scope is limited only by the inevitable concerns for conservation, energy use, and budget. In this chapter we review the range of opportunities that is made available by modern lighting equipment, while attempting not to get too involved in the details of lighting hardware. Developments in lamps and luminaires are occurring all the time, and for electronic controls, the pace of development is bewildering. This chapter seeks to describe generic trends in lighting controls, and readers who wish to acquaint themselves with the current state of display lighting technology will need to find their way to the appropriate websites and to open dialogue with the manufacturers and suppliers.

Light output control

There are just four basic types of light source that are commonly used for museum lighting.

Tungsten halogen lamps

The tungsten filament, electrically heated to incandescence, underwent a transformation in the 1950s with the invention of the halogen cycle. Its operating temperature had been limited to 2750K, but the halogen cycle enabled the filament to operate at higher temperatures, usually 3000K, but in some cases as high as 3200K. This gives more lumens per watt and a whiter light, and furthermore, it eliminates blackening of the inside of the lamp envelope, so that initial light output is maintained right up to end of life. Combining this development with low-voltage operation has enabled lamps to be miniaturized, with compact, robust filaments precisely located in small quartz envelopes. The advantage of small size is more than just space saving. Optical reflectors and lenses can redirect the emitted light with precision, giving improved performance in terms of both efficiency and light distribution control.

Facing page: *Fogg Art Museum, Cambridge, Massachusetts*

Nonetheless, incandescence unavoidably gives off more heat than light, and a maximum colour temperature of 3200K (or 3000K for many applications) is limiting. Colour temperature change filters can be added, but these produce higher colour temperatures by absorbing some of the power at the long wavelength end of the visible spectrum, further reducing efficiency. Even so, the modern 12 volt TH capsule, whether used with separate reflector or incorporated into an MR (multifaceted reflector) lamp, has established itself as a favourite for museum lighting and will be with us for some while. The MR lamps with 35 or 50 mm diameter dichroic reflectors are widely available in a range of wattage ratings and beam angles, and it may be noted that the familiar PAR (parabolic aluminized reflector) range of lamps has undergone significant development, with tungsten halogen and metal halide options, and smaller reflector diameters with more beam angle options. For precisely controlled narrow beams, the AR111 series (aluminium reflector, 111 mm diameter) provides a useful alternative integrated TH reflector lamp.

An attraction for all TH lamps is the ease with which light output can be controlled. They start instantly, and are dimmed simply by reducing the power supply voltage. This causes the lamp current to reduce, and enables light output to be smoothly reduced to extinction, without flicker. The most noticeable problem is colour change. Reduced light output is dependent on reduced filament temperature, so that the colour temperature of the emitted light is reduced by dimming. While at first a less noticeable effect, the halogen cycle operates only when the filament is close to its peak operating temperature, so that lamp blackening occurs when the lamp is dimmed.

Metal halide lamps

These high-intensity discharge lamps have undergone remarkable development in recent years. Their light output is produced by an electrical discharge in a confined arc tube that stimulates several halides, being binary compounds of one of the halogen elements, with each halide adding its own characteristic emission. While this has given the lamp manufacturers great scope to tailor light spectra, achieving colour consistency has been a long-running problem. The much higher luminous efficacy (lumens per watt) than is attainable from tungsten halogen has given the manufacturers the incentive to persist.

A major development has been innovative arc tube materials, particularly ceramics, which are relatively unaffected by the highly reactive conditions in the arc tube. This has led to more compact, short-arc sources, which operate at higher pressures and temperatures, enabling improved optical performance. Finally, the addition of rare earth materials to halides has contributed to the very good colour rendering that can be provided by modern metal halide lamps. Because each manufacturer employs its own blend of halides and other additives, it cannot be assumed that any MH lamps having the same colour temperature will appear similar or render colours in the same way.

The high luminous efficacy, choice of colour temperatures, and compact size of the modern MH lamp have made it an attractive option for many museum applications, including as the source for fibre-optic systems. To provide its designated light spectrum, the lamp must be operating at the correct temperature and pressure so that all components of the complex light production process are in balance. Dimming is used in some applications where the loss of colour rendering is acceptable, but it is not an option for museum lighting. Upon switching on, there is a warm-up period of several minutes before this occurs, and in the event of the lamp being switched off, there may be a delay of several minutes before it re-strikes.

Fluorescent lamps

The fluorescent lamp is a low-intensity discharge arc tube that is internally lined with a phosphor. The discharge produces predominantly short-wavelength UV radiation that is completely trapped by the glass tube, and which stimulates the phosphor to emit light which passes through the tube. By blending different phosphors, manufacturers can provide light of different colour temperatures, colour rendering properties, and luminous efficacies. Developments in phosphor technology have led to much improved colour rendering, and phosphors which operate at high luminance. This has led to slimmer linear fluorescent lamps and numerous configurations of compact fluorescent lamps, all of which are so bright that, for museum lighting, they must be treated as potential sources of glare and effectively shielded from direct view. Even so, their luminance is not high enough for them to be suitable sources for spotlights and other narrow beam optical systems, although they are useful for floodlighting and for spreading light over large surfaces, such as wall-washing applications.

The output of fluorescent lamps is not as easy to control as that of incandescent lamps, because the arc voltage has to be maintained while the current is reduced. This has become more easily achieved with the advent of electronic fluorescent lamp ballasts, so that dimming has become more commonplace. All types of linear fluorescent lamps, but only the four-pin types of compact fluorescent lamps, can be dimmed. The systems to achieve this range in complexity and cost, the less expensive systems permitting dimming down to around 10 per cent of full light output before flicker occurs, and the more expensive systems providing for smooth dimming down to around 1 per cent of full output.

Light-emitting diodes (LEDs)

The development of LEDs from tiny indicator lamps to high-intensity LEDs operating at one watt or more is a recent development, but already the attractions of this source have been noticed by museum lighting designers, and it must be expected that applications for this source will increase. Manufacturers have noted this trend in many markets, and are investing huge sums of money into LED development.

Basically an LED is a p-n junction which, when biased in the forward direction, becomes an efficient emitter of radiation, and currently there is a massive research effort to develop this device to produce useful quantities of visible light. An LED emits radiation in a fairly narrow spectral band, the peak wavelength depending upon the physical structure and materials used for the p-n junction. Each type of LED that emits in the visible spectrum has a characteristic colour, and always that colour appears saturated. White light can be produced in two ways: either by combining the outputs of three or more LEDs from different regions of the spectrum, or by using a blue or UV emitting LED to stimulate a phosphor.

LED output can be dimmed, but the process is different from conventional light sources. An LED is a low-voltage, direct-current device, and for it to operate, the voltage has to be maintained, otherwise it extinguishes. Fortunately, it can be switched very rapidly, and this is the key to achieving dimming. A control device generates a DC with a square waveform at a frequency too high to cause flicker (typically around 120 Hz) and dimming is achieved by pulse width modulation (PWM), which means controlling the ratio of pulse to gap duration.

Luminaire optical control

Lighting equipment used in museum galleries may be classified into three broad categories determined by luminaire optical control: spotlights, floodlights, and close-range applications. Optical control includes means of controlling the spatial distribution of light output, such as beam shape and avoidance of spill light; and also the spectral distribution of light output, such as the light colour and UV-blocking. Luminaire controls are taken to include effects of lamps with integral reflectors, and of attachments that may be added onto luminaires.

Spotlights

Spotlights incorporate reflectors or lenses or both to concentrate the lamp light into a beam. While this will have the effect of raising illuminance in a selected zone, skilful designers employ spotlights to fulfil specific lighting objectives. In Chapter 2 we examined how various object attributes may be revealed by lighting, and the use of spotlighting is associated particularly with providing lighting that has the quality of 'sharpness'. For objects that have appropriate attributes, lighting having the characteristic of 'sharpness' adds sharply defined highlight and shadow patterns to the illuminated appearance. Spotlighting can also generate attractive shading patterns, as distinct from shadow patterns, and where these are planned for consistency, a distinct 'flow of light' effect can be achieved.

A vast range of spotlights has been created for entertainment applications, and while it is only the least powerful of these that are suitable for museum use, there is an extensive choice of luminaires together with lighting control accessories that gives designers many opportunities for achieving their vision. Even the simplest form of spotlight becomes a versatile tool if, as illustrated in Figure 7.1, it is designed to house the entire range of tungsten halogen MR lamps, thereby giving a useful range of intensities and beam angles. For luminaires such as this, the lamp housing must be ventilated to cope with the IR heat that emerges through the back of the dichroic reflector, and the built-in electronic transformer may provide for dimming, either locally by a manual control on the luminaire or remotely by a control system. A glass filter is shown in front of the reflector, and there are two good reasons for ensuring that this type of luminaire is always operated with a hard glass UV-blocking dichroic filter in place. The first is that the quartz envelope of a TH lamp freely transmits short-wavelength UV, and although the amount of this radiation emitted by the filament is small, it has high damage potential. The other is that the TH capsule may shatter, and while the risk is low, the effect of a shower of hot lamp particles over a museum display could be devastating. Some MR lamps have integral glass covers, but it may not be possible to ensure that such lamps are always installed by maintenance staff. Spotlights of this sort may be ordered with a base for ceiling mounting, an adapter for attaching the luminaire to lighting track, or the type of hook clamp that is commonly used

Figure 7.1: *Typical spotlight for low voltage, tungsten halogen MR lamp. Selecon New Zealand Limited*

Figure 7.2: *Recessed spotlight housing. Selecon New Zealand Limited*

for stage and studio lighting. While these forms of mounting are good for access, the luminaires are entirely visible. Having them coloured to match the ceiling makes them less obtrusive, but there are recessing options that can make the luminaires quite inconspicuous (Figure 7.2).

While small, low wattage luminaires based on MR lamps may suffice for many museum lighting needs, larger spaces with longer light throws will call for more power, and for this we move on to a rather different type of spotlight. Figure 7.3 shows a typical Fresnel spotlight, this name coming from the inventor of the lens. Really, it is a plano-convex lens that has been compressed by having its thickness reduced in a series of concentric rings, while retaining its original contour in each of the separate segments. In the case illustrated, the housing can accommodate either a 70 W or 150 W single-ended metal halide lamp, or a tungsten halogen lamp in the range 300 W to 650 W. Behind the lamp is a spherical reflector, and the relative positions of reflector, lamp and lens can be adjusted to provide beam angles between 10 and 65°. The beam of a Fresnel spotlight will always have soft edges, but that can be changed by adding a 'zoom-spot' attachment (Figure 7.4). The advantage of zoom control is that as the beam is narrowed, the light gathered by the optical system is focused into the beam rather than being wasted, as happens with a diaphragm control. Slider controls enable adjustment of the beam angle and the beam sharpness.

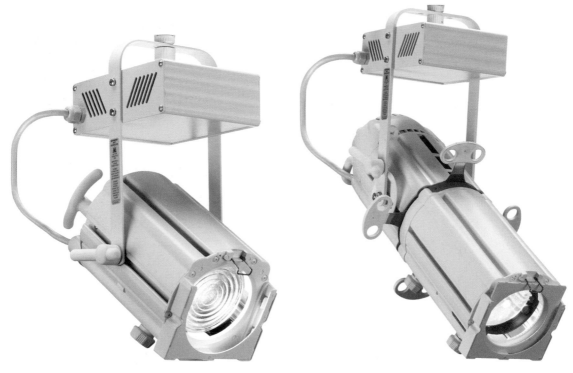

Figure 7.3: *Fresnel spotlight, for use with tungsten halogen or metal halide lamp. Selecon New Zealand Limited*

Figure 7.4: *Spotlight with 'zoom-spot' attachment. Selecon New Zealand Limited*

The extent of the versatility offered by spotlights becomes apparent when we review the range of attachments that is available. Commonly available attachments include:

- *Colour filters,* which are available in plastic or glass. Sheet plastic filters and gels impart colour by absorbing unwanted sections of the spectrum, whereas dichroic filters reject unwanted sections by reflection. Despite this difference, any colour filter in the focused beam of a spotlight can get very hot. Plastics are likely to have a short life, and annealed glass may crack, so that hard glass filters are usually recommended. Dichroic filters are the preferred choice for saturated colours. Colour filters are used only occasionally in museums, and then the most common use is to raise the colour temperature to blend with daylight.

- *UV-blocking filters,* and here again, there is choice between plastic, glass absorbing filters, and dichroic hard glass filters. As has been explained, the CIE defines the short wavelength end of the visible spectrum to be at 380 nm, while the UVA spectrum extends up to 400 nm. Conservators consider all wavelengths shorter than 400 nm to be UV, and they subject filter

Figure 7.5: *Spectral transmittance curves around 400 nm for several UV-blocking filters*

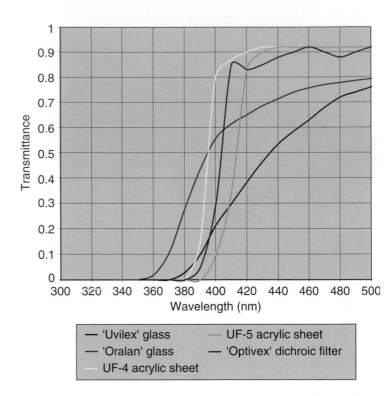

Figure 7.5: *Spectral transmittance curves around 400 nm for several UV-blocking filters*

spectral transmittance curves in this vicinity to careful scrutiny. Figure 7.5 compares some typical UV-blocking filters, where the ideal filter would zero transmittance below 400 nm, and total transmittance for longer wavelengths. No filters exactly achieve that sharp cut-off, but it can be seen that some come close to it. Those that eliminate all wavelengths below 400 nm tend to cut out some light at the short wavelength end of the visible spectrum, and this gives them, and the light they transmit, a yellowish appearance. On the other hand, filters that fully transmit all visible wavelengths down to 400 nm also transmit some of the UVA.

- *Diffusing filters,* which have the effects of softening beam edges and eliminating the appearance of striations in the beam pattern. It might be supposed that they would also have the effect of reducing the 'sharpness' of lighting, but as 'sharpness' is determined by the angular subtense of the light source, this will occur only if the filter has the effect of increasing the size of the source.

- *Spreader lenses,* which change a conical beam into an elliptical beam. It may be noted that when a conical beam is focused obliquely onto a surface, it forms an elliptical pattern. A spreader

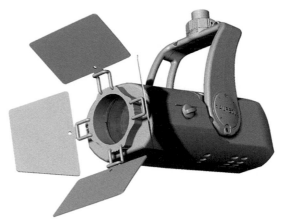

Figure 7.6: *Spotlight with 'snoot' attachment for reducing spill light. Selecon New Zealand Limited*

Figure 7.7: *Spotlight with 'barn-door' attachment for beam control. Selecon New Zealand Limited*

lens can be rotated to make the pattern more circular, or more elliptical.

- *Louvres,* which may be concentric rings or a honeycomb grill. They are used to reduce spill light, either for glare reduction or to avoid light falling onto adjacent surfaces.

- *Snoots,* being cylindrical attachments (Figure 7.6), are an alternative way of reducing spill light.

- *Barn-door attachments* support hinged 'doors' on a frame that can be rotated (Figure 7.7), enabling the 'doors' to be adjusted for blocking light within the beam that would fall outside the display area.

- *Beam-shaping attachments* incorporate a lens system to provide a sharply focused beam, with devices for precisely shaping the beam (Figure 7.8). These may include adjustable shutters, an adjustable diaphragm, or a gobo, this being a thin metal sheet from which the outline of the required beam shape has been cut by laser.

It is always advantageous to select a spotlight that will do the job with minimum need for dimming, and with minimum need for beam reduction by use of 'barn-door' or other accessories. This can be done by making use of the luminous intensity and beam angle data provided by the manufacturers, as illustrated by the following two examples.

Spotlighting a three-dimensional object

Figure 7.9 shows a statue to which we will apply spotlighting. We have selected a location for the spotlight that will generate attractive lighting patterns, and we want to select a suitable MR lamp. The ambient light level in this space is 75 lux, and we decide on a 2:1 ratio for the sculpture, which means that we are to add another 75 lux. At first the technical data on these lamps appears intimidating, and it helps to organize the data as shown in Table 7.1.

We start by choosing a beam spread. It can be seen that the choice comes in quite large steps, so we do not need high precision to make the appropriate selection. The distance from the spotlight to the object $d = 3.8$ m, and at this distance, we need a beam diameter (2 × radius) $2r = 1.5$ m. The beam angle that we require must not be less than:

$$B = 2 \tan^{-1}(r/d)$$

$$= 2 \tan^{-1}(0.75/3.8) = 22°$$

From Table 7.1, the 24° beam angle will suit us well. Now we turn attention to luminous intensity required, and for this we apply the inverse square law. For I = luminous intensity, and E = illuminance:

$$I = E/d^2$$

$$= 75 \times (3.8)^2 = 1080 \text{ cd}$$

From Table 7.1, we select the 20 W 24° lamp. As this lamp has a luminous intensity of 1200 cd, the maximum illuminance on the statue due to the spotlight will actually be 83 lux.

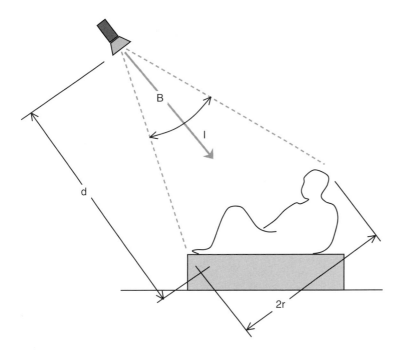

Table 7.1 *Typical data for 12 volt tungsten halogen MR lamps with 50 mm diameter dichroic reflector*

Watts (W)	Luminous Intensity (candelas)	Beam angle (degrees)
20	4200	10
	1200	24
	560	36
35	7200	10
	2000	24
	1200	36
50	10 000	10
	3100	24
	1800	36
	800	60

Spotlighting a two-dimensional object

Figure 7.10 shows a section through a museum space in which a painting, measuring 0.9 m high and 0.6 m wide, is hanging on the wall. The aim is to mount a luminaire with an MR lamp onto the ceiling to bring its illuminance up to 200 lux. The ambient light level is 75 lux, so the spotlight is to add 125 lux.

Figure 7.10: *Spotlighting a two-dimensional object*

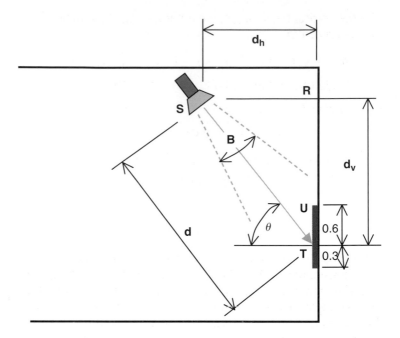

Figure 7.10: *Spotlighting a two-dimensional object*

To direct the spotlight onto the centre of the picture would give a noticeably uneven illuminance distribution, and it would be better to direct the beam centre to a point two-thirds of the way down the picture. Keeping in mind the discussion in the previous chapter concerning avoidance of veiling reflections, it is decided to make the horizontal distance out from the wall $d_h = 3.1$ m, and allowing for the projection of the luminaire below the ceiling, the vertical distance $d_v = 4.4$ m. Then the distance from luminaire to picture:

$$d^2 = (d_h)^2 + (d_v)^2 = (3.1)^2 + (4.4)^2 = 29.0 \, \text{m}^2$$

$$d = 5.4 \, \text{m}$$

For determining the required beam angle, we have to take account of the angle at which the beam strikes the picture. The situation that we want to ensure is that the upper corners of the picture are within the beam angle, but to calculate this angle precisely would be tedious. The simple approach is to calculate the beam angle required both horizontally and vertically, and then to allow a bit for the corners. The horizontal beam angle is easy, so we will do that first.

$$B_h = 2 \tan^{-1} 0.3/5.4 = 6.4°$$

For the vertical beam angle, we determine the half angle above the beam centre:

Angle RST $= \tan^{-1} (d_v/d_h) = \tan^{-1} 4.4/3.1 = 54.8°$

Angle RSU $= \tan^{-1} (4.4 - 0.6)/3.1 = 50.8°$

Angle UST $= 54.8 - 50.8 = 4.0°$

$$B_v = 2 \times 4.0 = 8.0°$$

The 10° beam angle MR lamp would work well in this application. The luminous intensity required:

$$I = E \times d^2$$
$$= 125 \times 29 = 3625 \, cd$$

We choose the 20 watt 10° beam angle MR lamp which will give a small amount of spill light onto the wall surrounding the picture, and if undimmed, would provide 145 lux on the picture. These two examples make the point that for spotlighting in museums, low-wattage lamps are sufficient for many applications. By selecting the right lamp for the job, the dismal effect of low colour temperature due to lamps being dimmed to run far below their rated output can be avoided.

Floodlights

Floodlights really are the basic units of museum lighting installations. Their purpose is to provide washes of even illumination within the space, and designers use them to set the scene. The appearance of the walls and the ceiling, and the ambient illumination in which the displays are set, are balanced to the brightness of the displays by controlled floodlighting. The balance achieved, and how this varies from space to space within the museum, is a crucial design decision, quite apart from being instrumental for achieving progressive adaptation.

Although a floodlight may appear to be simply a lamp in a glass-fronted box, it is again the optical design that is vital for producing a useful lighting tool. The unit shown in Figure 7.11 gives an asymmetric beam to spread light evenly over extended surfaces, and it provides this distribution with soft beam edges to enable the beams from adjacent luminaires to overlap without noticeable effect. It is shown with a 'barn-door' attachment, and while other accessories such as filter holders are available, the range is much less extensive than for spotlights. Powerful floodlights using high-intensity discharge lamps are used wherever light is to be spread across large areas, and again, for museums, we are concerned with

Figure 7.11: *Floodlight with 'barn-door' attachment.*
Selecon New Zealand Limited

the very lowest light outputs. This is an application that particularly favours linear lamps rather than compact sources, and 4-pin compact fluorescent lamps, which are capable of dimming and offer a choice of colour temperatures, can be used very effectively. However, tungsten halogen lamps, in mains voltage or low voltage, continue to find favour despite their low efficacy and low colour temperature. The ease with which dimming can be controlled is a major factor, although it is generally recommended that it is better to change to a lower wattage lamp than to dim to a low level and suffer from very low colour temperature.

Floodlight luminaires usually permit a choice of lamp wattage, but determining the appropriate lamp wattage for a particular application by calculation involves an additional step that we do not need to bother about for spotlight applications. As we raise the light level of a surface that forms a substantial proportion of the total room surface area, the increase in illuminance is due to the sum of effects of both direct and inter-reflected light. The direct light calculations are as for spotlights, and predicting the effects of inter-reflections is dealt with in Chapter 8.

The wall-washer is a special type of floodlight that does not provide for tilt. This is because the luminaire optics have been developed to

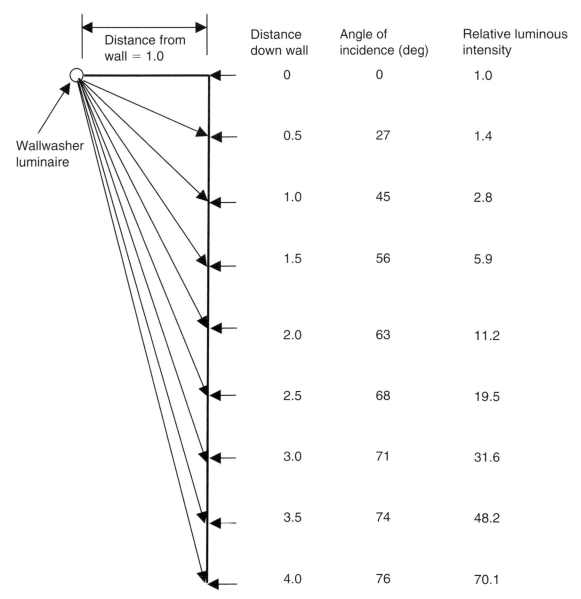

Distance down wall	Angle of incidence (deg)	Relative luminous intensity
0	0	1.0
0.5	27	1.4
1.0	45	2.8
1.5	56	5.9
2.0	63	11.2
2.5	68	19.5
3.0	71	31.6
3.5	74	48.2
4.0	76	70.1

provide a uniform illuminance distribution over a flat surface (wall-washers can be mounted on the wall to illuminate a ceiling) and this requires precise control of the luminous intensity distribution in the vertical plane. Figure 7.12 shows the relationship between distance out from the wall for a ceiling mounted wall-washer and the relative luminous intensity distribution required for uniform illuminance down the wall. It is essential that wall-washers are installed strictly in accordance with the manufacturer's instructions, and it can readily be seen why wall-washers are generally not recommended for more than 3:1 wall/ceiling distance ratios.

Figure 7.12: *Relative luminous intensity distribution for a 'wall-washer' luminaire to provide uniform wall illuminance. It is impractical to aim for uniform wall-washing for down wall/from wall ratios of more than 3:1*

Close-range applications

It often happens in museums that lighting occurs at close range, and this raises problems of avoiding excessive local brightness and light exposure, and achieving a satisfactory illuminance distribution over the display area. This likely to occur where lighting is required to be installed inside display cases or underneath shelves. The compact light sources discussed in the previous sections give the wrong light distribution, and while fluorescent lamps may give the right type of distribution, they emit far more light than is usually needed and have to be operated substantially dimmed. Fortunately, two relatively new types of lighting are well suited to close-range lighting applications.

Fibre optics distribute the output from a single high-power light source to a multiplicity of outlets, each of which can be independently aimed and, with the right equipment, focused. Figure 7.13 shows a display case in a space that has ample ambient illumination, and there are four fibre-optic outlets inside the case. As we draw close, the useful functions served by these outlets become apparent. Figure 7.14 shows an iron helmet, which actually is a

Figure 7.13: *Display case with fibre optics lighting in 'The Vikings' Exhibition. With permission, National Museum of Denmark. Auckland Museum, Auckland, New Zealand*

Figure 7.14: *Iron helmet, showing use of fibre optics lighting to create highlight pattern to reveal surface qualities (with permission, National Museum of Denmark, Auckland Museum)*

replica based on fragments of a tenth century Viking helmet, and the effect of the close-range lighting in revealing the sheen of the metal and the contrast of the visor decoration is evident. Even more notable is the appearance of Viking axe head show in Figure 7.15. Made of iron, it is intricately inlaid with gold and silver wire and pins in patterns of a tree and birds. This is an example of where highlights due to source-surface-eye geometry count for far more than illuminance, and close-range lighting can enable designers to optimize this type of situation. Another example of fibre-optic lighting is shown in Figure 6.60.

Light-emitting diodes (LEDs) are making inroads into close-range museum lighting applications, as their small size, low heat emission and long life are favourable characteristics. Figure 7.16 shows an example of LEDs being used in amiable luminaries which can be fitted with a choice of lenses to give a range of beam spreads.

Figure 7.15: *Gold and silver inlaid axe head with detail revealed by fibre optics lighting, from 'The Vikings' Exhibition (with permission, National Museum of Denmark, Auckland Museum)*

Figure 7.16: *A Maori genealogy staff (Rākau whakapapa) from 1800 to 1900, with close range display lighting from LED sources (with permission, Museum of New Zealand/Te Papa Tongarewa)*

The displayed object is a nineteenth century Maori genealogy staff, and this illustration shows how controlled light beams in a close-range application, combined with low surface reflectances, can be used to isolate an object and make it appear to float in space. However, some caution needs to be applied when the use of LEDs is being considered. In the case shown, 'white' LEDs are used, but their colour rendering is likely to be found unsatisfactory where the colour appearance of dyes or pigments is crucial. An alternative approach to providing white light from LEDs is to employ a combination of sources, each contributing to a different waveband of the visible spectrum. While good colour rendering could be provided in theory, practical application of this approach would depend on being able to maintain the balance of components as the LEDs undergo different rates of ageing. LEDs are currently undergoing intensive development, and it is to be expected that they will replace traditional light sources in many applications. While there are difficulties to be overcome, LEDs would appear to be particularly well suited for close-range applications in museums.

Luminaire directional control

Locating, aiming, and focusing luminaires is the lighting designer's ultimate act in setting up a lighting installation, and loss of these adjustments is the most common cause of deterioration and failure during the life of the installation.

Lighting track affords designers a level of freedom to locate luminaires for optimum direction onto exhibited objects. Figure 7.17 shows part of an installation where light track beams span between parallel rows of fixed track, enabling luminaires to be located at any point on the ceiling. Track lighting systems are generally designed to enable luminaires to be easily detached from lighting track and relocated, and also to be realigned for changing displays by simply taking hold of the luminaire and swinging it to a new direction. This flexibility can be more of a curse than a blessing in museums.

Figure 7.17: *A connecting lighting track strut between runs of recessed track enables spotlights to be located at any point on the ceiling. Arthur M. Suckler Gallery, Washington, DC*

Figures 7.18 and 7.19 show two views of a spotlight luminaire specifically designed for museum lighting. After aiming the luminaire, the designer locks both the pan and tilt movements with an Allen key. Filters, lenses, and beam control attachments fitted in front of the lamp are left undisturbed when lamp changes are made, as this is done through the back of the luminaire. In these ways, the lighting designer is able to exercise long-term control over these essential aspects of lighting control.

Lighting control systems

Recent developments in control systems have been, in a word, astounding. It is now possible for luminaires capable of emitting hundreds of thousands of lumens to be remotely controlled for

Figure 7.18: *Directional adjustments on a spotlight being locked with an Allen key (with permission, Mike Stoane Lighting)*

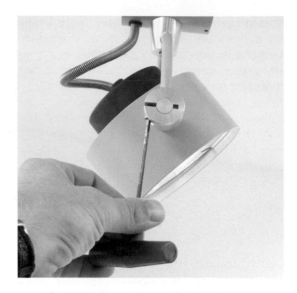

Figure 7.19: *Lamp changing through the back of a luminaire leaves attachments undisturbed (with permission, Mike Stoane Lighting)*

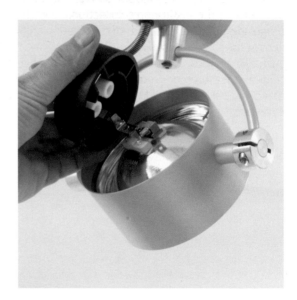

light output, including flashing effects; light colour ranging from white to saturated colours; beam angle; and beam direction both in pan and tilt; and for dozens of such luminaires to programmed for choreographed effects. All of this makes the demands of museum lighting seem quite modest.

There really is no point in trying to give a summary of current practice because it will be obsolete by the time this book is published. Instead I will give a personal view of what may be the potential for lighting control systems in museums.

Modern control systems can enable every luminaire to be individually addressable and, providing the lamp type and control gear are suitable, adjusted for light output. In this way, the lighting for any display area, or even individual objects, can be automatically controlled for time of day or availability of daylight.

It also means that when setting up a new display lighting installation, the designer would be able to adjust the light outputs using an infrared or wireless remote control. While walking through an exhibition, the designer would be able to adjust every luminaire seeing the displays from a visitor's viewpoint. It would be possible for the control system to save several settings, any one of which could be recalled by an operator selecting a preset button, or by having time-controlled slow fades between different scenes.

Lighting control systems will increasingly become integrated components of overall management systems, taking care not only of building factors such as indoor climate and security, but also management of the institution's collection. From there it is a natural progression to having records of the location and condition of every item in the museum's collection augmented with records of cumulative light exposure. The ability to relate these records to reflectometry measurements recording the changing states of displayed objects could greatly add to our knowledge of the effects of light exposure.

Lighting strategies 8

Even when we have all the principles well in mind, there are many totally different ways in which a design solution can take form.

Ambient illumination

John Boud has commented that 'lighting for effect could almost be defined as lighting that is incomplete by intent', and has recalled: 'I remember Douglas Charters being asked, after a lecture many years ago, how you should light a painting. "Put it in a well-lit room," was the reply. At the time I thought this was cynical; now I suspect it is accurate' (Boud, 1971). There is plenty of scope to discuss exactly what is a well-lit room, but I think we can safely assume that what was meant was a room in which illumination is plentiful and of good colour rendering, shadows are soft, and there are no spots of glare or areas of gloom. Figure 8.1 shows a gallery where, arguably, these conditions pertain. Everything is well lit and clearly visible: the walls, ceiling and floor; the stairs and handrail; and the paintings. Viewers should feel that they have really seen the paintings, as everything would be visible: the brushstrokes; the layering of

Figure 8.1: *High room surface reflectances for the 'well-lit room' at the Walker Art Center, Minneapolis, Minnesota*

Facing page: *Isabella Stewart Gardner Museum, Boston, Massachusetts*

Figure 8.2: *Very low ambient illumination for 'glowing in the gloom' for this display of Japanese kimonos at the Museum of Natural History, Washington, DC*

pigments and varnishes; perhaps some canvas showing through; and any effects of ageing, such as surface cracking and fading. All would be visible.

It is just a coincidence that the complete opposite of the 'well-lit room' has been described by one of Boud's work associates, Derek Phillips:

> During a visit to Woburn Abbey I found that in one room, which is full of paintings by Caneletto, each individual painting had been lit using framing projectors through pin-holes in the ceiling, leaving the rest of the room in comparative darkness. My first reaction was one of enjoyment, but the more I looked at these Canelettos the more nasty they appeared. They seemed to be giving off light like a coloured slide. . . (Phillips, 1971)

Phillips' experience is an extreme case of displayed objects 'glowing in the gloom', and while he described the appearance of the paintings as 'nasty', such a response is not inevitable when this type of display is employed. When the Museum of Natural History, Washington, DC, presented a collection of Japanese silk kimonos, they needed to reveal the rich colours and deep textures of fabrics. However, dyed silk is notorious among fugitive materials, and the museum staff no doubt felt themselves duty-bound to restrict light exposure as much as possible. A large gallery was completely blacked out, and within it, some of the kimonos were arranged sequentially (Figure 8.2) and others individually (Figure 8.3), with the lighting always directed from above and restricted to the displays with minimal spill. The ambient illumination was very low, so that once viewers were adapted to the surrounding gloom, the displays were in

Figure 8.3: *An individual kimono on display at the Museum of Natural History, showing the effect of 'sharpness' of lighting*

high contrast with their surrounds and imparted sensations of intense colour, even though the display illuminance levels were severely restricted. Furthermore, the low ambient illumination caused the directed display lighting to produce high vector/scalar ratios, causing the deeply textured fabrics to generate strong shading patterns and produce a striking visual experience. This is an example of what Boud meant by lighting that is 'incomplete by intent'. Certain attributes of the displayed objects have been selected for emphasis, and not everything is equally visible. The effect is striking, but it is a contrived effect. The exhibition designer has decided what is to be the appearance of these objects, and the entire setting, including the lighting, has been assembled to present viewers with this visual experience.

These two lighting conditions, the 'well-lit room' and 'glowing in the gloom', are two extremes of a continuum, and between these extremes there are many levels at which designers can balance ambient and display lighting. It should, however, be apparent that the difference between these conditions has less to do with how the displayed objects are lit than with how the surrounding space is lit. It is, therefore, entirely appropriate that before a designer thinks about lighting the objects, thought is given to the appearance of the space.

The notion of a 'well-lit room' suggests an experience that is comfortable and reassuring, particularly if the architecture forms a setting that is conducive to a positive overall experience. Viewers are free to direct their gaze to what catches their attention, and perhaps to find their own way through the displays. However, as ambient illumination is reduced, so opportunities increase for the exhibition designer to direct their gaze, and even their movements. It is not just the objects to be seen that are made visible, but the selected visual attributes of those objects that can be promoted to attract attention. It is not just a matter of being able to give these objects higher brightness, but being able to make them appear more colourful, or more glossy, or to reveal subtle characteristics such as opalescence, or sheen, or clarity. Meanwhile, features that are deemed to be irrelevant or potentially distracting, which probably will include the architecture, recede into the gloom.

The technical aspects of ambient illumination have been covered in some detail elsewhere (Cuttle, 2003), but still it is instructive to engage in a thought exercise. If we switch on a lamp in the middle of a room, and the lamp emits 1000 lumens, how much light do we have in the room? All of the light emitted from the lamp lands on room surfaces, and if we assume all of those surfaces to have a uniform reflectance of 0.5 (i.e. 50 per cent of incident light is reflected and the remainder is absorbed), then 500 lumens are reflected back into the room. So, after this 'first bounce', we have 1500 lumens in the room. If we follow these reflected lumens, they too are incident on room surfaces, and so after their second bounce, we have 1750 lumens in the room. These successive reflections occur until the number of lumens becomes disappearingly small, at which time we can estimate the total number of lumens by multiplying the initial lumens (the output of the lamp) by $1/(1 - R)$, where R is the room surface reflectance. As $1/(1 - 0.5) = 2$, it can be seen that by having room surfaces that reflect back half of light incident upon them, we have doubled the amount of light in the room. If this seems surprising, consider the effect of increasing the reflectance. If $R = 0.8$, then $1/(1 - R) = 5$, so now we have increased the incident light five-fold! Clearly, white paint can make an enormous contribution to energy-efficient lighting, but is this the reason why it is so popular in art galleries? Well no, there is a different reason for that.

Think of our room having totally black surfaces, so that $R = 0$. In this case, $1/(1 - R) = 1$, so that the initial lumens equals the total lumens. If our room has a total surface area of 100 square metres, the average illuminance of the room surfaces equals 10 lux, as 1 lux = 1 lumen per square metre. How well lit would this room appear? The lamp would appear glaringly bright, but the room surfaces would be completely dark. It is obvious that the room appearance depends on the inter-reflected lumens, that is to say, the lumens that have undergone their first and subsequent bounces. We have an illuminance of 10 lux on the room surfaces, and a light meter would show this, but we have no reflected light and no ambient illumination. To cope with this situation we change the expression to $R/(1 - R)$, as this revised expression provides us with a measure of the interrelationship reflected light and direct light. For the black room, $R/(1 - R) = 0$; for $R = 0.5$ it returns a value of 1; and for $R = 0.8$ it returns a value of 4, and these values indicate the ratio of inter-reflected light to direct light. It shows us the enormous effect of room surface reflectances, and this is important because the inter-reflected light is the ambient illumination. It is this that determines adaptation level, and makes all the difference between a 'well-lit room' and 'glowing in the gloom'.

In Chapter 2 we discussed the illumination engineering the term exitance, which is the number of lumens per square metre (lm/m^2) emerging from a surface (see Figure 2.2). The mean room surface exitance (M_{rs}) provides the measure of ambient illuminance, and returning to the example of the room in which the average direct illuminance is 10 lux, when $R = 0$, $M_{rs} = 0$; when $R = 0.5$, $M_{rs} = 10\,lm/m^2$; and when $R = 0.8$, $M_{rs} = 40\,lm/m^2$. It is a simple matter to explore the effect of other room reflectance values, remembering throughout that the initial lumens is 1000 lm and the room surface area is 100 m^2.

The concept of mean room surface reflectance is very valuable for assessing the effect of lighting on the appearance of a museum space. The fact that we may be putting a lot of light into a room does not mean that it will appear well lit, nor does the illuminance incident onto the room surfaces give us a reliable indication. What matters is the amount of indirectly reflected light within the space. Suppose that we are aiming to achieve a 'well lit room', then it makes sense to direct the initial lumens onto large surfaces which have high reflectance values. Alternatively, consider a space in which only the displays are to receive direct illumination. What balance between display and ambient illumination will be achieved? Just because only the display materials receive direct illumination does not necessarily mean that the ratio will be high, and designers should be aware of what are the influential factors. The light reflected from the displays is the first reflected flux (FRF), or the 'first bounce lumens', and provides the initial lumens for the inter-reflection process. The number of these lumens depends on three factors: the display illuminance (E_d), the illuminated display area (A_d), and the reflectance of the display materials (R_d):

$$FRF = E_d \times A_d \times R_d \text{ lm}$$

What level of mean room surface exitance (M_{rs}) will be produced by these lumens? That depends on two factors: the room surface area (A_{rs}), and its reflectance (R_{rs}):

$$M_{rs} = FRF/ (A_{rs} (1 - R_{rs})) \text{ lm/m}^2$$

These are the governing principles, and hopefully this thought exercise will assist designers to visualize the situation that they are creating. To apply these principles for predictive calculation it is recommended to refer to Cuttle (2003).

Before leaving this topic, consider how you might measure mean room surface exitance. You do not measure the illuminance on the room surfaces. Instead, satisfy yourself that you have a reasonably typical view of the space, and hold the light meter directly in front of your eyes and normal to your direction of view. Now make sure that direct light from luminaires and windows is shielded from the meter, and also from light directly reflected from displays, so that the meter is exposed only to reflected light from the room surfaces. It may help to mount the meter on a tripod, ensuring that it is at eye level and angled to measure illuminance on a vertical plane. Take your reading in lux, and this measure should give you a reasonably representative value of the mean room surface exitance in lm/m^2.

The extent to which display lighting catches attention and directs people's viewing depends upon the display/ambient illuminance ratio, although of course other factors will be influential. The ratios in Table 8.1 may be applied as a general guide.

Table 8.1 *Perceived differences of illuminance*

Perceived difference	Illuminance ratio
Noticeable	1.5:1
Distinct	3:1
Strong	10:1
Emphatic	40:1

A sequence of visual experiences

Ken Gorbey, a New Zealand museum designer, has explained to me that a visit to a museum or art gallery should be like reading a good novel, with change of pace and occasional surprises. There should be times when one is encouraged to linger and contemplate, and other times when one is drawn through rapidly changing surroundings.

Art museums have traditionally provided for a procession, usually by planning the galleries on a symmetrical grid with connecting archways aligned to give a series of enfilades (Figure 8.4),

Figure 8.4: *A series of enfilades at the New South Wales Art Gallery, Sydney, Australia*

Figure 8.5: *The National Gallery of Canada, Ottawa, with the entrance at the near corner and the Grand Hall at the far end*

and within this framework the gallery staff can arrange displays around whatever themes are appropriate, for the viewers have little opportunity to deviate from the prescribed path. This possibly could achieve Gorbey's concept, but some designers have set out to create settings that make a celebration of the sequential experience.

At the National Gallery of Canada, architect Moshe Safdie could be seen to have composed a preamble. The entrance is located at a corner of the museum site that connects to a busy city square (Figure 8.5), and from here, visitors ascend an 80 m long ramp with a 5.5 per cent gradient (Figure 8.6). This leads to the Grand Hall, being the tall crystal-shaped structure seen to the left of Figure 8.5, and from this elevated position the visitor has a view over the adjacent streets to the Canadian Parliament Buildings, which are located on a bluff on the bank of the Ottawa River, and beyond to Quebec Province (Figure 8.7). This clearly is a place to linger, not only to admire the view but the space itself. The translucent triangular sails at the top of the structure are computer-controlled to respond to sunlight, and there is something organic about this response. Safdie has said of this space, 'I wanted to create the feeling you get when you are under a tree, which is one of the nicest feelings in the world.' The whole procession is preparation for entering the gallery, and by policy, no artworks are displayed along the route. At this point, visitors are likely to be adapted to very high brightness levels, and so from here a further transitional space leads them away from the light and towards the middle of the building, and to the upper level of galleries.

Figure 8.6: *The approach to the Grand Hall at the National Gallery of Canada*

Arthur Erickson handled the entering experience rather differently at the University of British Columbia Museum of Anthropology. A winding path leads visitors to a simple post and beam construction entrance which opens to a lobby, from which the way forward is down a dimly lit ramp that forms a tunnel-like gallery, but there is light at the end of the tunnel (Figure 8.8). The first glimpse of what is in store gives an impression of being led out of the museum and into open landscape (Figure 8.9), but as visitors emerge, they become aware of being in an

Figure 8.7: *Visitors pause in the Grand Hall at the National Gallery of Canada*

enclosed space, but one that is minimally separated from the outdoor environment by a large expanse of apparently unsupported west-facing glazing (Figure 8.10). Within this space the great totem poles and other carved and painted wooden figures of the native people of Canada's west coast can be seen in almost unattenuated daylight while being protected from weathering. The element of surprise is heightened by the fact that, unlike at Ottawa, visitors are given no hint of what awaits them.

Figure 8.8: *Visitors are led into the Museum of Anthropology, University of British Columbia, Vancouver, by a view of 'light at the end of the tunnel'*

Figure 8.9: *As visitors advance, the view through a glazed wall opens at the Museum of Anthropology*

Figure 8.10: *Visitors emerge into the main hall of the Museum of Anthropology, where there is minimal obstruction to daylight or view through the vast glazed aperture*

Figure 8.11: *'The Friendly Alien' that is the Kunsthaus at Graz, Austria*

Surprise has become an architectural feature among some recent art museums. The Kunsthaus has acquired the nickname 'The Friendly Alien' among the citizens of Graz, and one could readily believe that a being from another world has landed in this historic town (Figure 8.11). The architects, Peter Cook and Colin Fournier, cause visitors to enter the alien from below, ascending through its skin on a 'Pin', this being a moving floor that connects ground level to Space 02 (Figure 8.12). At this level visitors are fully enclosed within the alien, with no views to the outside and totally reliant on electric lighting, but another pin leads up again to Space 01 (Figure 8.13). Here the visitors are conscious of being under the bulging upper surface of the alien with its protruding nozzles (Figure 8.14). The dark interior surfaces keep the ambient illumination levels low, and the flow of light formed by each nozzle is expressed in outline first by hoops of white neon lighting, and then by truncated funnels of grey fabric. These divide the space into separate display settings, each defined by its own pool of light. The atmosphere is introverted and intense, but then for relief, one can wander through to the 'Needle', this being a glazed platform offering extensive views over the old town.

Progression through the galleries of a museum will inevitably present a variety of visual experiences. The differences of scale and content of the exhibits cause viewers to change their pace

Figure 8.12: *Visitors enter the Kunsthaus from below on an ascending 'pin' that takes them to the lower of two exhibition floors*

Figure 8.13: *Another 'pin' takes visitors to the upper floor at the Kunsthaus*

as they respond to the displays, and the variation of lighting from the 'well-lit room' to the 'glowing in the gloom' experience plays an important role in evoking these responses. Also, there are simple ways of punctuating the progression through a

Figure 8.14: *At the upper floor level of the Kunsthaus, the nozzles that are such a feature of the exterior are found to be sources of daylight, reinforced by rings of neon and cones of fabric*

Figure 8.15: *Visitors are likely to pause at this point of their journey, at the Portland Museum of Art, Portland, Maine*

museum and instigating a change of pace. Figure 8.15 shows a space along the route through an art museum. It would take a totally committed art viewer not to pause here for a while, and to sense the recession of museum fatigue as one enjoys the visual contact with the outdoors. It may be noted that in most other situations, restfulness and relaxation are associated with relatively low light levels, which makes this role of lighting in museums unusual, if not unique.

Figure 8.16: *The first sight of Michelangelo's* David *is at the end of a gallery containing several of the master's sculptures, at the Academia, Florence*

Alternatively, the progression can be punctuated with an exclamation mark, in the form of an icon. Seen from afar, Michelangelo's *David* is instantly recognizable and rivets attention as it draws the crowds (Figure 8.16). Both placement and lighting are crucial. David had been brought to the Academia, which formerly had been an art school, from the Piazza del Signoria in 1873. It had stood in the piazza for more than three and a half centuries and had suffered from more than just weathering. During a riot, a substantial part of David's left arm had been broken off, and clearly this pride of the city, seen to characterize the Florentines' self-image of youthful spirit in the face of an overbearing force (Rome), needed more than mere protection. It is located so that visitors approach David through a long gallery flanked by six of Michelangelo's sculptures, and which leads to the junction of ways where the statue stands. The dome that provides the flow of diffused daylight was constructed to receive David, and he stands slightly back from the

Figure 8.17: *The dome that provides the daylight 'flow of light' was specially constructed to receive the icon*

Figure 8.18: *The setting encourages visitors to walk around the statue, and its location gives distant views from several directions*

centre of the dome, so that the illumination vector direction is inclined towards his body. The view when approaching through the long gallery is the familiar frontal view, washed by the flow of light. Drawing closer, the lighting reveals the translucency of the polished surface of the marble, and the form of the youthful, muscular body is thrown into relief. In fact, even the hairline crack in the carefully repaired left forearm is quite discernible. For me, the experience of a visit is memorable for being able to make one's way right around the sculpture, and to see its changing posture from all angles (Figures 8.17, 8.18).

The Louvre also provides an outstanding example of presentation of an icon. When first seen, *Winged Victory* appears to have

Figure 8.19: *A distant view of* Winged Victory *at the Louvre, Paris, framed by the architecture and lit by a dome skylight*

been given the status of an object of devotion (Figure 8.19), but upon drawing closer it is seen to be on a busy intersection (Figure 8.20). It is located at a point where visitors will be passing from one zone of the museum to another, and returning to the metaphor of the novel, it marks the closing of one chapter and the opening of another. Anyone moving through this area passes close to the statue, and can hardly fail to be moved by the experience of this gem of Greek sculpture and the beautiful flow of daylight that reveals it (Figure 8.21). It may be noted that the *Mona Lisa*, probably the world's most famous picture,

Figure 8.20: *The location of* Winged Victory *at a meeting of ways gives alternative views of the sculpture*

is hanging not far away, and for many visitors this will be a prime objective of their visit. It undoubtedly has iconic status, but it cannot serve a similar role in the sequence of visual experiences. Its size, its two-dimensional form, and the fact that it has to be protected by massively strong security glass, all make it a terminal point rather than an event along a route.

Of course, not many museums have the advantage of instantly recognizable icons, but nonetheless, the combination of location and lighting can achieve considerable effect with unfamiliar artefacts. At Castelveccio, Carlo Scarpa presented visitors with an enfilade (Figure 8.22), but there was nothing to prepare them for the impact of the view shown in Figure 8.23. This is unquestionably an event along the route, and we should take a careful look at this view. While the daylight is diffused, the moderately low surface reflectances ensure that the flow of light is distinct. The direction of flow is from the left at approximately 45°, a condition favoured for artists' studios. This light washes over not only the displayed objects, but also the textured wall surfaces. It may be asked: Is it the light that reveals the texture, or is it the texture that reveals the light? The directional lighting

Figure 8.21: *The downward flow of diffused daylight interacts with* Winged Victory *to create distinct shading patterns*

effects on the objects could be provided by spotlights, so what would be the difference? Although the source of light is not visible, it is unmistakably daylight. We recognize it not because of its intensity or its colour characteristics, but by coherent flow of light within this space. It is that flow, revealed by the textured walls, that creates the *gestalt* that is a daylit space.

These examples have shown non-responsive objects on permanent display, and in every case, the setting is a 'well-lit room'.

Figure 8.22: *An enfilade of galleries at Castelveccio, Verona, Italy*

The wish to achieve high visual impact for responsive objects often leads designers towards low ambient illumination settings, to enable high contrasts to be achieved with restricted display illuminance, and examples of this are described in Chapter 6. A consequence of this approach is that museum spaces having architectural merit may become unrecognizable, but this may be shrugged off with the retort that the visitors have come to see the displays, not the décor. This attitude may be carried through to exhibition designers wishing for nothing more than totally dark space in which they can practice their magic, so that they can create virtually any visual effect in any space. Not unnaturally, this does not please architects, and some have responded in an assertively positive manner.

Architect Hans Holein was faced with an acutely triangular site for the Frankfurt Museum of Modern Art. He responded by placing the entrance on a corner (Figure 8.24), and leading visitors up through the museum on a winding staircase that presents a new surprise at every turn (Figures 8.25 to 8.32). He has provided the exhibition designers with a succession of varied and irregular spaces, and at the time of my visit, these designers had responded by arranging art to suit the settings. It probably would be quite impractical to mount an exhibition on

Figure 8.23: *The placement of objects to be framed by an archway, and for lighting patterns to be generated by the 'flow of light', at Castelveccio*

a chronological or a theme basis, but the designers clearly had achieved successes in exploiting the settings to give impact to the presentation of art, and certainly, they had provided an intriguing sequence of visual experiences.

Figure 8.24: *The Frankfurt Modern Art Museum, Frankfurt, Germany, is on a triangular site with the entrance on the near corner*

Figure 8.25: *A visit to the Frankfurt Modern Art Museum starts at a ground level display space, and leads to the stairs at the middle of the building*

Figure 8.26: *From the bottom of the stairs, there is a view into a tall, narrow gallery*

Figure 8.27: *Ascending the stairs gives intriguing views into other gallery spaces*

Figure 8.28: *A balcony gives a another perspective of the tall, narrow gallery*

Figure 8.29: *The stairs lead on, with more views into surrounding spaces*

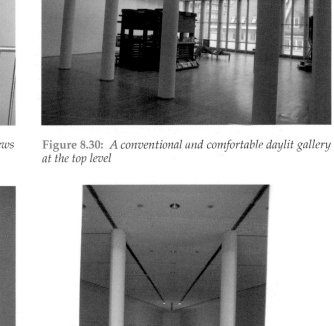

Figure 8.30: *A conventional and comfortable daylit gallery at the top level*

Figure 8.31: *The entrance to a very unconventional gallery nearby, glaringly lit by fluorescent lamps*

Figure 8.32: *Descending back down the stairs, every gallery space is seen to have a fresh and individual character, in this case lit only by tungsten halogen spotlights focussed onto the display objects*

Figure 8.33: *This museum for old documents is an adapted small church, which provides a fitting and pleasant setting for visitors. St Peter Hungate, York, UK*

Minimal-exposure displays

There are some time-honoured methods for reducing the damage caused by light exposure which rely on minimizing the duration of exposure. Figure 8.33 shows a medieval setting in which old books and manuscripts are displayed in lectern cases. These cases are fitted with dark blue velvet curtains over the glass covers that are above the more delicate objects, and these curtains are drawn aside by the viewer (Figure 8.34). Another approach that is quite often encountered in churches in Mediterranean countries is a 'pay as you go' approach. Many of the artists in the Renaissance era were commissioned by churches, and notable works hang in the churches to this day. To ensure that visitors who come to see the art rather than to pray make some contribution towards the upkeep of the church, the lighting for the artworks may be controlled by coin-slot time switches. I have found that one Euro usually buys around five minutes operation of a nearby floodlight, as shown in Figure 8.35.

It is usually the policy in museums for all displays to be operational all the time that the museum is open for viewing, so that controlling the exposure of responsive materials has to be effected by restricting display illuminance levels, as has been explained in Chapter 3. To achieve satisfactory displays at low illuminance, it is essential that the exhibition designer understands the role of visual adaptation and employs it effectively in planning the route that visitors will take to reach these displays.

Figure 8.34: *Exposure of these rare books is restricted by velvet covers, which have to be lifted for viewing the documents. St Peter Hungate, York*

Sometimes museum staff demand that it should be possible to display any object at any position within the museum, but it has to be expected that such an approach will produce visually unsatisfactory results.

As has been explained in Chapter 2, in museums we are concerned with visual adaptation within the photopic range, which is the range of vision that depends upon the responses of the retinal cones. We need the cones to be fully operational for us to have a satisfactory level of ability to discriminate detail and colour, and for this to happen, there must be sufficient light arriving at the eye. It is usual for conservators to specify light levels in terms of illuminance, whereas it should be obvious that it is not the light incident on the object that affects how well it may be seen, but the light reflected from the object towards the viewer's eyes. As has been discussed, illuminance times reflectance equals exitance, so that exitance gives us the measure of density of reflected light in lumens per square metre.

For photopic vision, an exitance of $10 \, \text{lm/m}^2$ is required. If a person having normal visual ability is adapted to this level of light from objects in the field of view, then that person should be able to discriminate moderately fine detail in the objects, and if the colour rendering of the incident light is satisfactory, they should also be able to discriminate fairly small colour differences. The levels of discrimination ability for this condition are not maximum or even optimum, and certainly someone working on repair or restoration of the object would demand far more light. What we are providing for museum visitors is sufficient light to enable discrimination at a level where further reduction of incident light would lead to a marked deterioration of discrimination ability. What is meant by normal visual ability has been discussed in Chapter 2.

To work out how much illuminance we need to achieve an exitance of $10 \, \text{lm/m}^2$, we need to know the surface reflectance. It might be supposed that a surface of mid-lightness would have a reflectance of around 0.5 (i.e. 50 per cent of incident light is reflected), but in fact, we would judge a grey surface of this reflectance to be light grey. A mid-grey surface typically has a reflectance around 0.2, meaning that 80 per cent of incident light is absorbed. So what illuminance do we need to provide in order to achieve an exitance of $10 \, \text{lm/m}^2$ from a mid-lightness surface? The answer is that the illuminance must equal $10/0.2 = 50$ lux, and here we have the illuminance value that is widely recommended as the maximum level for displaying moderately and highly light-responsive museum objects. Some

Figure 8.35: *The spotlight illuminating this painting has been activated by a coin-operated switch, at San Giorgio Maggiore, Venice*

people mistakenly suppose that it is a safe exposure level, but this is not so. It is simply the illuminance below which visual discrimination ability is likely to suffer for materials that appear at least as light as a mid-grey surface. It has been widely adopted as the recommended limiting illuminance for both moderately and highly responsive objects, the difference being that it is recommended that highly responsive objects are not placed on permanent display.

The 50 lux limiting illuminance has become something of a universal mantra among museum staff. Illuminance meters are reasonably affordable and require a minimum of skill to operate, whereas there are no simple equivalents for measuring exitance. However, it should be obvious from the foregoing that the illuminance that is actually needed to provide satisfactory visual conditions depends on the reflectance of the illuminated object. It is a matter of readily confirmed observation that for paintings that are displayed under restricted light levels, details may be hard to discriminate in areas of dark colours, while areas of light colours may gain an enhanced contrast. The appearance of such paintings would benefit from more light. On the other hand, the appearance of works on white paper with light colours probably would suffer little from having the illuminance reduced, with the benefit being less light-induced damage. To treat all objects as mid-lightness surfaces keeps life simple, but if the objective is to satisfy visual needs with minimum exposure, the right solution is to provide just adequate exitance. Meanwhile, it must be appreciated that the exitance that would be judged just adequate depends on the viewer's state of visual adaptation.

It is a common experience that when walking indoors from bright sunlight, there is a noticeable period within which the room appears dim and colours appear dull. The duration of this period increases as we get older, as the process of visual adaptation slows down. Rather more dramatic is the reverse effect. After a period out of doors at night, we may find that entering a room and switching on the light causes a brief period of discomfort or even pain, causing us to shield our eyes from the glare. Although light adaptation may impinge on our consciousness more than dark adaptation, it is a much quicker process. Either way, the process involves the retinal receptors adapting their sensitivities to the overall exitance of the surrounding field. The range from bright sunlight to starlight is vast (in the order of ten million to one) and far too big for the eyes to cope with simultaneously. Once we have adapted to a condition, we can cope readily and comfortably with a range of around 100:1. While the previously mentioned experiences tell us about adaptation, they are far more extreme than anything that we encounter in well-designed museums.

All museums want the first experiences of visitors to be inviting and pleasant, so that entrance halls are generally well-lit, whether by daylight or electric lighting. Visitors are often confronted by a variety of eye-catching features, such as promotions of forthcoming events, retail sales, and the museum café. At this point, they are adapted to moderately high exitance values, that is to say, lower than outdoor sunlight, but far above 10 lm/m². To lead visitors directly from this condition to minimal-exposure displays would be grossly unsatisfactory. They need a route that progressively reduces their adaptation level, so that when they reach the displays they are adapted to ambient levels less than the display levels, so that the displays appear as brighter elements within their field of view.

The previous section discussed procession through a museum, and this provides the opportunity for reduced adaptation to be achieved progressively. It is usual for visitors to enter the galleries at the lower level, although there are exceptions (e.g. the Kimbell Art Museum, the National Gallery of Canada), and where this occurs, it can greatly assist progressive adaptation. Visitors move from the entrance hall into daylit galleries, and progress down stairs to more enclosed spaces where light levels, as well as other environmental factors, may be more readily controlled.

There is, however, a remaining difficulty in encouraging visitors to progress in this way. The phenomenon of phototropism refers to the tendency for a person's direction of view to be attracted towards the brightest part of the surrounding field, and as this part becomes the area of attention, so it is likely to attract the person to move in that direction. Particularly where museums offer visitors a choice of routes to follow, there is a difficulty in attracting visitors towards minimal-exposure displays.

A first step to overcoming this is to avoid the enfilade of galleries. Upon entering the gallery shown in Figure 8.36, there is no choice of ways ahead, but as we progress down the gallery we become aware of the strategically placed and selectively illuminated statue in the space beyond (Figure 8.37). This attracts our attention and, hopefully, our wish to proceed, even though it is obvious that we will be moving into an area that has a lower ambient light level. This approach can be developed into a series of galleries in which the view from each gallery to another gallery reveals a feature, which may be architectural or an artwork, and which acts as a way-finding device. After visitors have moved into a new space, their next set of choices is revealed to them. This planning approach gives much opportunity for progressive adaptation. The perceived differences of illuminance listed in Table 8.1 may be referred to for general guidance.

Figure 8.36: *From this gallery, the route proceeds to zones of lower ambient illumination. The National Museum of Canada, Ottawa*

Figure 8.37: *Statues have been located to draw attention, and one has been placed to be framed by the archway that leads to the lower ambient illumination zones. The National Museum of Canada, Ottawa*

When the Museum of American History, Washington, DC, decided to place its collection of the First Ladies' Gowns on permanent display, the conservators specified a maximum illuminance of 35 lux. These gowns, which had been worn by successive Presidents' wives at Presidential Inaugural Balls, starting with Martha Washington, form the centrepiece of an exhibition which reviews various ways in which First Ladies have acted their roles, some choosing to make their marks as hostesses, others as promoters of culture, or advocates of social causes, or as political partners. As visitors make their way through these displays, they follow the twisting route shown in Figure 8.38, which leads them towards the hall where the gowns are displayed. The resident lighting designer, Edwin Robinson, employed this convoluted route to progressively reduce visitors' adaptation levels. Ambient illuminance levels are shown on the figure,

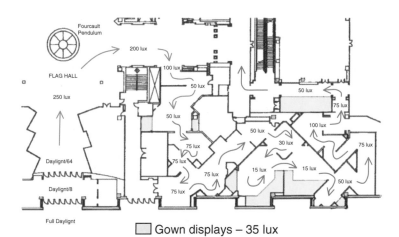

Figure 8.38: *The progressive adaptation route that visitors to the Museum of American History, Washington, DC, have to follow to in order to be able to see the 'First Ladies' Gowns' exhibition*

Figure 8.39: *The central display area of the 'First Ladies' Gowns' exhibition, illuminated to 35 lux in a space where the ambient illuminance is 15 lux*

and visitors were led from the Flag Hall, with its famous Star Spangled Banner display and an ambient illuminance of 250 lux, to the gowns hall where the ambient illuminance was a mere 15 lux. The central section of this display, illuminated to 35 lux by dimmed incandescent lamps, is shown in Figure 8.39.

Barry Gasson's 'Walk in the woods' at the Burrell Collection has been mentioned (see Figure 4.91). The first sighting that visitors have of what is in store is a glimpse through a medieval archway (Figure 8.40), and it draws like a magnet. Once inside and fully adapted to this daylit space, there is a choice of avenues leading back, away from the woodland view and into the heart of the museum (Figure 8.41). There are walkways with skylights which lead through the building, offering views into the gallery spaces, and there are archways, each leading to a series of galleries with

Figure 8.40: *The first glimpse that visitors have of the 'walk in the woods' at the Burrell Collection, Glasgow, UK*

Figure 8.41: *From the woodland view space at the Burrell Collection (see Figure 4.91), visitors have the choice of following daylit walkways that connect through the museum or moving into spaces with progressively reducing ambient illumination*

Figure 8.42: *From within the low ambient illumination spaces, visitors have glimpses back to the daylit zones*

Figure 8.43: *Inside the low ambient illumination spaces, these displays of medieval tapestries receive controlled levels of display lighting*

Figure 8.44: *This illuminated graphic at the Getty Center, Santa Monica, California, draws visitors towards the gallery in which Getty's collection of Old Masters' drawings is displayed at restricted illuminance levels*

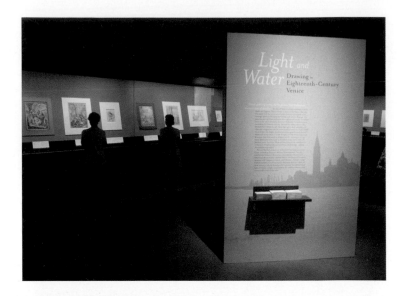

Figure 8.45: *The fibre-optics outlets that illuminate these drawings from above are totally concealed by the display cases. The vertical glazing and sloping display surfaces are arranged so that the drawings, many of which contain fine detail, may be viewed from close range. The Getty Center*

progressively reducing light levels. Taking this latter option, one can glance back to the daylit space (Figure 8.42), and then look around the enclosed galleries (Figure 8.43). The Burrell has a notable collection of medieval tapestries, remarkable for the fact that the range of original dye colours is largely preserved. These are displayed under carefully controlled lighting conditions, but even at this distance from the outside walls, there are glimpses of daylight, in this case through a medieval clerestory.

Works on paper are a major source of concern for conservators. The Getty Center's collection of Old Masters drawings is displayed in cases that support the works at eye level, and provides

Figure 8.46: *A detail view of the Getty Center display cases. Veiling reflections are absent in this view, although some veiling reflections do occur where cases face each other*

illumination by a totally concealed fibre-optics installation. A selectively illuminated panel is located to attract visitors' attention as they approach from adjacent galleries (Figure 8.44), and to provide a transitional brightness as they enter the gallery. Once within, visitors complete adaptation to the low ambient light level, and the displays, for which illuminance is precisely regulated, appear to be quite acceptably bright (Figure 8.45). In some instances, parallel cases face each other and reflections in the glazing are noticeable, but where this does not occur, the glass appears to disappear (Figure 8.46).

The great space

The construction of the Aswan High Dam on the River Nile threatened a number of ancient Nubian monuments, and a massive international effort to save the most significant of them from being flooded by Lake Nasser was coordinated by UNESCO. In 1965, the Egyptian Government gave the Temple of Dendur to the American people as a mark of thanks for their contribution to the rescue effort. The temple had been erected on the banks of the Nile by the Roman emperor Augustus around 15 BC, during his occupation of Egypt and Lower Nubia, and was due to be flooded on completion of the dam. It was awarded to the Metropolitan Museum of Art in 1967.

While the museum had lobbied hard for this treasure, the task of housing a sandstone temple complete with its gateway in an existing museum would have seemed daunting. To meet this need, the Sackler Wing was constructed which provided not

Figure 8.47: *The great space that houses the Temple of Dendur at the Metropolitan Museum of Art, New York*

merely sufficient space, but a great space in which to exhibit the temple. As visitors passing through the Egyptian section of the museum enter the space, they find themselves confronted by a moat (Figure 8.47), the edge of which represents the Nile bank, and set back at the correct distance from the bank stands the gateway to the temple. Daylight floods into the space from a huge glass wall that opens onto Central Park, and after crossing the moat, visitors gain a sense of the scale of the temple due to the spaciousness of the enclosed space and the strong visual contact with the outdoors (Figure 8.48). It may be noted that the strong flow of light from the glass wall has been softened by counteracting use of electric lighting. The interior of the temple also has electric lighting (Figure 8.49), but the overall effect is an open, airy space in which daylight flows across the monumental stonework, playing on its forms and revealing the bas-relief carvings (Figure 8.50).

Not many museums have the opportunity to construct a great space, but sometimes the opportunity comes when a large building is converted to become a museum. The Parisian railway station, the Gare d'Orsay, underwent several temporary uses after trains ceased to call, before it was slated for demolition.

Figure 8.48: *Visitors wander around the Temple of Dendur, that is visually connected to Central Park by a vast glazed wall*

Figure 8.49: *While the illusion is somewhat reduced by the electric lighting inside the temple building, the daylight 'flow of light' interacts strongly with the three-dimensional forms*

Figure 8.50: *Detail of the bas relief carvings on the Temple of Dendur*

The ensuing public outcry prompted a political directive that it be transformed into a museum, and under the direction of interior architect Gae Aulenti, the railway hall once again became a great space. The glazed arched roof imparts a sense of light and spaciousness to visitors entering the museum beneath the monumental hanging clock, seen at the far end of the hall in Figure 8.51. Galleries opening off to both sides of the central aisle are used for moderately responsive objects, such as oil paintings, and passing through these spaces leads to galleries with more restricted light levels and where more responsive objects may be displayed. Above these galleries are open walkways which, like the central aisle, are devoted to sculptures, and at this level there are many vantage points for viewing artworks in a memorable setting (Figure 8.52).

Another opportunity occurred when the Battersea Power Station on London's South Bank became redundant and was taken over by the Tate Gallery to exhibit modern artworks. The cavernous space of the old Turbine Hall has become the outstanding feature

Figure 8.51: *The old railway hall of the Musée d'Orsay, Paris, provides spacious accommodation for the Central Aisle, and the sculptures that it houses*

Figure 8.52: *Routes through the Musée d'Orsay break into the hall at higher levels, giving visitors new perspectives of the space and providing more opportunities for large works to be displayed*

Figure 8.53: *The old turbine hall of a power station provides a grand space for the Tate Modern, London*

of the Tate Modern (Figure 8.53). At first it is a space to get lost in, and then the sculpture is found (Figure 8.54). It is simply washed with the pervading daylight, and attracts no attention other than by its own presence. It can be walked around and viewed from all directions, as if it were located out of doors, rather than in the sheltered environment of a museum.

For the Sainsbury Centre for the Visual Arts, architect Sir Norman Foster created a single great space for the entire museum. The building, which has rather unkindly been likened to an aircraft hanger, has 30 m wide by 7.5 m high clear glass end walls (Figure 8.55), and in addition, daylight is admitted through translucent panels in the roof, and is moderated by electrically controlled louvres at ceiling level (Figure 8.56). The triangulated welded steel trusses that provide this column-free space are 2.4 m deep, and all building services, including electric lighting, are housed within their depth. The resulting sense of openness and uncluttered space is evident, but it brings a problem. In order to display light-responsive objects it has been necessary to construct enclosures (which have been likened to bus

Figure 8.54: *Large sculptures can be experienced in an environment that gives shelter to the artworks, while retaining some outdoor visual qualities. The Tate Modern*

Figure 8.55: *The steel trusses that form the Sainsbury Centre for the Visual Arts span 35 m and provide 7.5 m clear height. All building services, including the lighting, are housed within the depth of the trusses*

shelters) to attenuate the light level (Figure 8.57). In this great space, there is no opportunity for achieving progressive adaptation. The display system has been designed to relate to human scale, as the collection, which had been a gift from Sir Robert

Figure 8.56: *Daylight ambient illumination is automatically controlled by motorized louvres at the level of the underside of the trusses, in the Sainsbury Centre for the Visual Arts*

Figure 8.57: *An area of restricted illumination for displaying responsive materials, at the Sainsbury Centre for the Visual Arts*

and Lady Sainsbury, had been assembled in their home, and the sizes of the objects reflect this. Some non-responsive objects are given a lighting boost from spotlights above the 7.5 m ceiling level (Figure 8.58), but objects that are too responsive to withstand the ambient illumination have to be shielded.

The way in which visitors are exposed to this great space achieves significant impact. The museum is part of the University

Figure 8.58: *Detail of a sculpture in a display cabinet at the Sainsbury Centre for the Visual Arts. Supplementary electric lighting for local emphasis and 'sharpness' is provided from the services zone overhead*

of East Anglia campus, which has an elevated walkway that connects buildings above the vehicular traffic level. This enables visitors to enter through the side of the building, just below ceiling level, and the entire museum interior is spread out before them, although they are not encouraged to linger here as the narrow walkway connects directly to an elegant spiral staircase leading down to floor level (Figure 8.59). If we return to the novel metaphor, the effect of one of these great spaces is a high impact, which may occur in the opening chapter, or as in the case of the Temple of Dendur, as a major event within the text.

It may be noted that the previous photographs of the Sainsbury Centre were taken in 1987, ten years after it opened, whereas Figure 8.59 was taken on a more recent visit. The appearance of the space is more grey, and I had the impression that the controls had been set for a lower level of overhead daylight illumination. Perhaps this reflects a change of policy at the museum, although the staff present could not confirm this. However, it brings to mind the observations of the staff at the Lentos Museum (Figures 4.43–46), who maintain ambient light levels well in

Figure 8.59: *Visitors to the Sainsbury Centre for the Visual Arts who arrive from the University of East Anglia's elevated walkway enter the gallery just below daylight control louvres, and they see the entire museum spread out beneath them, before they descend this spiral stairway to the museum floor level*

excess of the levels recommended by conservators because they have found that their spacious galleries, illuminated by diffused light, need moderately high light levels if they are not to appear dull, or worse, gloomy. It may also be noted that the exhibition of Japanese kimonos staged by the Museum of Natural History, Washington, DC (Figures 8.2–8.3), was in a large space, but there was no sense of it being a great space. The space was lost in the gloom, but this was by design. The gloom was as important as the spotlighting to make the kimonos glow. It is evident that to be effective, a great space has to be a 'well-lit room'.

Visual connections

The inherent difficulty of attracting people to progress from a bright environment into a dim one has been discussed, and

Figure 8.60: *This route through the Museum of Modern Art, New York, provides a visual connection to the outdoors, and visitors take the opportunity to linger*

strategies that may help to overcome this reluctance have been described. There is another closely related difficulty. It is sound policy for museum staff to locate fragile and fugitive objects remote both from windows and from the external skin of the building, as this enables more precise control of environmental conditions. This can mean that many of the most precious objects that a museum has on display are in galleries that are not only cut off from daylight and outdoor views, but which also impart a sense of enclosure that even people who are not susceptible to claustrophobia may find disagreeable. The use of low ambient light levels to enhance the appearance of displays at restricted illuminance values adds to this unwanted effect.

At the Museum of Modern Art, New York, a series of electrically lit galleries displays works of the early modernists from the museum's permanent collection with due attention to illuminance restrictions. The openings between galleries are arranged to give through views, and from a distance, a horizontal band of glazing is visible, and through it, a view of foliage (Figure 8.60). The window head is low and the surrounding buildings high, so there is no view of sky. Paintings are set well back from the window, and even the sculpture placed where it would catch any light from the window needs spotlighting. The range of brightness is comfortable, but still, the window acts like a magnet for visitors who are starting to sense the museum fatigue effect, and they settle on the strategically placed seating.

This device of providing galleries for minimal-exposure displays with visual connections to the outdoors can be achieved by suggesting the connection, without admitting a significant quantity of daylight or even providing an outdoor view. The photo of the

Figure 8.61: *This space at the Gulbenkian Museum, Lisbon, has restricted display illuminance, and offers glimpses through to daylit spaces*

Figure 8.62: *These windows do not permit a view to the outside, but nonetheless they provide an unmistakable daylight connection. The Auckland Art Gallery, Auckland, New Zealand*

tapestries on display at the Burrell Collection (Figure 8.43) shows this well, and at the Gulbenkian Museum the sense of enclosure is greatly mitigated by the side windows which are fitted with neutral grey glass (Figure 8.61). The windows at the Auckland Art Gallery (Figure 8.62) have diffusing fabric blinds, and these

Figure 8.63: *The central atrium of this museum has no daylight or view to the outside, but visual connections to other galleries give a sense of spaciousness. Rijksmuseum Vincent van Gough, Amsterdam*

controls do not aim to reduce brightness down to the adaptation level determined by the electric lighting, but rather to suggest visual connections to a brighter space beyond the gallery. Daylight has symbolic value, but visual connection can be effectively achieved within galleries that are largely or even completely dependent on electric lighting. At the Rijksmuseum Vincent van Gough, a central atrium provides visual connections between differently illuminated galleries (Figure 8.63) in a way that is reminiscent of the Yale Center for British Art (Figures 4.101–4.103).

Courtyards offer a range of opportunities for visual connections. The Freer Gallery was built in the 1920s in classical style around a spacious square courtyard. A corridor overlooking the courtyard provides the principal circulation route, and the effect of the diffused daylight from central skylights is often enlivened by connecting views from the galleries to the courtyard (Figure 8.64). By modifying the proportions and surface reflectances of courtyards, designers have opportunities to provide visual connections to daylit spaces that do not need tinted glass or translucent blinds to moderate brightness. At the National Gallery of Canada,

Figure 8.64: *The Freer Art Gallery, Washington, DC, is built around a square courtyard and visitors have frequent views into the courtyard as they make their way between gallery spaces*

Moshe Safdie provided two courtyards for the two storeys of galleries. Figure 8.65 shows the view through to the Water Court at the lower level. It may be noted that the central skylight also provides daylight, and as described in Chapter 5, this is achieved by light ducts from roof level. This approach of visually changing an enclosed space by linking it to a courtyard can be particularly effective in small spaces. The appearance of the small gallery at the Queensland Art Gallery shown in Figure 8.66 is quite transformed by the view through the glass end wall, which opens to an outdoor space that is merely 1.2 m wide.

The provision of visual connections between enclosed galleries and more open spaces is likely to be a concern where ambient light levels in the enclosed space have to be low, and of course, these are the situations in which it requires care to obtain a balance that provides an effective connection but which does not detract from the appearance of the space or the displays. Conversely, there are situations where electric lighting provides moderate light levels and the space may be enlivened by substantial visual connection directly to the outside, as at Museé l'Orangerie, where this central Parisian gallery exploits its adjacency to the

Figure 8.65: *This space is on the lower of two gallery floors at the National Gallery of Canada, Ottawa. The central skylight is connected to roof level by a light duct (see Figures 5.3, 5.4), and the courtyard provides another form of connection to daylight despite distance from the outside*

Figure 8.66: *A narrow outdoor space transforms the appearance of this small gallery space at the Queensland Art Gallery, Brisbane, Australia*

Figure 8.67: *The galleries at Musée l'Orangerie, Paris, are lit by fluorescent lamps above the laylight, but wall space has been sacrificed in order to visually connect the galleries to the adjacent Tuileries Gardens*

Figure 8.68: *The Kroller-Muller Museum, Otterlo, the Netherlands, is located in a large park. This gallery for non-responsive materials exploits the potential for visual contact*

Tuileries Gardens (Figure 8.67). Even so, nothing matches the level of visual connection that can be achieved when a museum located in a large park has a gallery devoted to works that are non-responsive to light exposure, as at the Kroller-Muller Museum (Figure 8.68).

Procedures for practice   9

Every museum needs a policy for limiting the light exposure of exhibits and ensuring adequate illumination for safe use of the building. The first section of this chapter gives a pro forma for such a policy which is broadly in line with the recommended practice documents listed in the Bibliography. It is intended that this pro forma could form the basis of a lighting brief for a new museum, or for renovation of an existing museum. Alternatively, it could provide a basis for a museum's in-house lighting policy, or for instructions to an exhibition designer. Whichever way it may be used, it is recognized that the institution concerned will need to adapt the document to suit its own circumstances. The aim of this pro forma has been to provide a comprehensive coverage of museum lighting issues, so that any institution that uses it will be alerted to the full range of lighting concerns.

Exhibitions designers and museum staff with responsibility for lighting sometimes find it difficult to comply with a lighting policy while also meeting expectations for providing excellent viewing conditions for the exhibits, and this is particularly likely to occur where a decision is made to display responsive objects in or adjacent to a location of high ambient illumination. This issue is addressed in the sections that follow the pro forma, which deal with setting up lighting for a new display, and monitoring the lighting during the time that the objects remain on display. The approach taken is to encourage museum staff to apply limiting exposure rather than limiting illuminance recommendations.

A museum lighting pro forma

Lighting functions

In all exhibition spaces, the lighting systems must provide separately for the following lighting functions.

During exhibition hours
Ambient lighting is required to provide general illumination in every space sufficient to ensure safe use of the building. According to

location, the ambient lighting may also reveal the architecture and provide some, or all, of the display illumination. A system of electric lighting is required to provide ambient lighting in all exhibition spaces, although it may not be operational for much of the time in some daylit spaces. The overall light level is to be adjustable up to an illuminance determined by the lighting category (see following text), but generally the relative distribution of ambient lighting within the space is expected to remain more or less constant.

Display lighting is required to enable exhibition designers to give emphasis to particular exhibit attributes, such as three-dimensional form, or surface texture, or gloss. While display cases may have their own built-in lighting, the installed display lighting refers to directional lighting that is adjustable for both direction and intensity. Designers are to have the freedom to set the balance of ambient and display lighting to suit circumstances, so it is recommended that all display areas should be provided with both systems. In this way, designers can decide whether the role of the display lighting is to provide selective emphasis within an adequately lit environment, or to be the sole source of exhibit illumination.

Out of exhibition hours

Cleaners' lighting is required to enable the floors to be cleaned. The cleaners do not touch the exhibits, but they may be required to clean surfaces of glazed showcases that can be touched by the public. Cleaners' lighting is to be provided by an unobtrusive installation of luminaires that directs its light output onto the floor and avoids direct illumination of exhibits. It is to be used only while cleaning is in progress.

Security lighting is required to enable security cameras to operate and security staff to move through the building as required. This lighting is controlled from the security room, and very little light is needed. The most important aspect for the cameras is to provide a well-diffused distribution of light that avoids strong shadows and reflections of light sources in shiny surfaces.

At all times

Emergency lighting is to be available to provide for safe egress from the exhibition spaces in the event of failure of the electricity supply. This lighting has to comply with appropriate codes and standards.

Whereas the electric lighting could be designed as five independent systems, opportunities for sharing functions should be considered. For example, it may be practical to utilize the emergency lighting luminaires to provide some of the security lighting. Even so, care must be taken not to compromise the functions. In particular, it should be expected that exhibitions designers will set the ambient lighting in some galleries to light levels which are below the level required by the cleaners, and the display lighting should not be used to make up the difference.

Requirements for the Cleaners' lighting, Security lighting, and the Emergency lighting are given on p. 274. The following two sections deal with the ambient and the display lighting requirements.

Responsiveness categories

The four responsiveness categories defined by the CIE were introduced in Chapter 3. These categories have been classified as R0 to R3, and for convenience, Table 3.3 is reproduced below as Table 9.1. Advice on identifying museum materials and classifying them for responsiveness is given on p. 275.

Table 9.1 *Limiting illuminance (lux) and limiting annual exposure (lux hours per year) for material responsiveness categories*

Material responsiveness categories	Limiting illuminance (lx)	Limiting exposure (lx h/y)
R0. Non-responsive	no limit	no limit
R1. Slightly responsive	200	600 000
R2. Moderately responsive	50	150 000
R3. Highly responsive	50	15 000

Lighting categories

Four lighting categories are defined which are identified as L0 to L3 according to the level of control. These categories define the lighting performance to be achieved by the ambient and the display lighting in combination, and they relate to increasing levels of overall environmental control. A higher lighting category means that light exposure may be more precisely controlled, and this should correspond with spaces where other environmental factors, such as temperature and humidity, may also be more precisely controlled.

The basis of this specification is that lighting categories range from L0 to L3, and material responsiveness categories range from R0 to R3. The following sections describe these categories and their relevance to museum lighting.

Designers should not lose sight of the fact that it is generally desirable that visitors enter exhibition spaces through galleries that have controlled admission of daylight and some opportunities for visual contact with the outside, and that as they progress into the building, their visual adaptation will gradually and imperceptibly be reduced to the low illumination levels demanded for responsive exhibits. Consistent with this is the concept that spaces that are more remote from the 'skin' of the building will have more precisely controlled environmental conditions. Visitors will move through spaces that are better suited for display of slightly or moderately responsive exhibits to reach spaces that provide the full range of precisely controlled environmental conditions demanded by lending institutions for highly responsive exhibits. It is with these concerns in mind that guidance is included for both physical and visual connections for each lighting category.

This section should be read in conjunction with Figure 9.1. The principal outcomes are summarized in Table 9.2.

Lighting category L0: Uncontrolled daylight

Lighting category L0 is daylight without illuminance control. The daytime appearance of an L0 exhibition space should be light, airy, and spacious, with a clear sense of outside visual contact. While this category of environmental control is often associated with entrance foyers and circulation areas where exhibition may be a secondary function, it may include spaces where exhibition is the primary function.

Exhibits Objects intended for permanent exhibition in an L0 zone need to be composed entirely of materials having R0 category (Table 3.1), or alternatively, they may comprise materials that are renewable or replaceable. Such materials would include living plant material, samples of common minerals, or temporary exhibition materials produced specifically for display, with the intention that they will be discarded when they have fulfilled their purpose.

Physical connections An L0 zone may connect to the outside, and will connect to L1 or perhaps L2 zones. It will not connect directly to an L3 zone.

Visual connections The sense of visual contact with the outside should be strong in an L0 zone, implying side glazing and access to a significant outside view. Internal views into L1 and/or L2 zones are intended to arouse anticipation and to provide visitors with clear indication of how to progress towards the principal exhibition spaces.

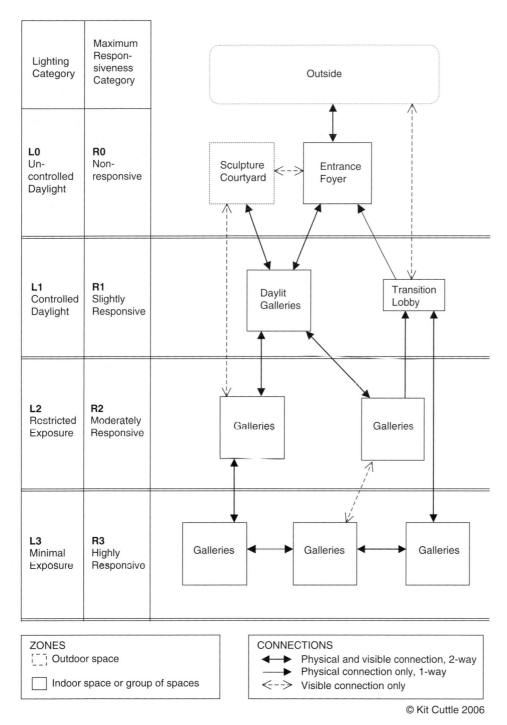

Lighting Category	Maximum Responsiveness Category
L0 Un-controlled Daylight	**R0** Non-responsive
L1 Controlled Daylight	**R1** Slightly Responsive
L2 Restricted Exposure	**R2** Moderately Responsive
L3 Minimal Exposure	**R3** Highly Responsive

Outside

Sculpture Courtyard

Entrance Foyer

Daylit Galleries

Transition Lobby

Galleries

Galleries

Galleries

Galleries

Galleries

ZONES
⌐ ¬ Outdoor space
▭ Indoor space or group of spaces

CONNECTIONS
◄──► Physical and visible connection, 2-way
───► Physical connection only, 1-way
◄--► Visible connection only

© Kit Cuttle 2006

Figure 9.1: *Connections between zones corresponding to the pro forma museum lighting policy.*

Table 9.2 *Summary of principal factors relating to the ambient and display lighting systems in the exhibition spaces*

Lighting category	**L0** Uncontrolled daylight	**L1** Controlled daylight	**L2** Restricted exposure	**L3** Minimal exposure
Maximum material responsiveness category	**R0** Non-responsive	**R1** Slightly responsive	**R2** Moderately responsive	**R3** Highly responsive
Daylight admission	Yes		No	
Sunlight admission	Yes	No		
Exposure limit (lx h/y)	No limit	600 000	150 000	15 000
Illuminance limit (lx)	No limit	See text	50	
Colour Rendering Index (CRI)	CRI ⩾ 85			
Correlated Colour Temperature (CCT)	2900K < CCT < 4200K			
UV control	No	Yes		
IR control	No		Yes	

Daylight *Glazing:* Side glazing with access to a significant outdoor view is recommended. Neutral grey tinted glass may be used, particularly adjacent to L2 zones, although such glazing should be avoided at entrances as it presents a visual barrier to prospective visitors. There may be overhead skylight glazing in addition to side glazing.

Sunlight admission: Occasional shafts of sunlight are permissible, but solar heat gains are to be restricted whether or not these zones are within the air-conditioned volume.

Daylight distribution: This will vary according to outdoor conditions.

Illuminance control: Illuminance will vary according to outdoor conditions, but the overall extent of daylight is to provide a visual transition between the outdoors and the controlled illuminances of L1 and L2 zones.

Ultraviolet control: Not required.

Electric light *Duration of use:* There will be minimal daytime use of electric lighting, although some selective display lighting may be employed. For night-time, ambient and display electric lighting are required.

Light distribution: The main purpose of the ambient electric lighting system will be to reveal the architecture and to provide an attractive appearance, both from inside and outside, when daylight fades. It may satisfy the need for cleaners' lighting. A flexible system of display lighting is required except in locations where it has been decided that there will be no display.

Illuminance control: The ambient and the display lighting systems are to be separately controlled. The ambient lighting system control is to enable a smooth transition between daytime and night-time conditions. The display lighting system control may provide for continuous adjustment as ambient lighting conditions change.

Colour rendering: General Colour Rendering Index to be not less than 85.

Colour appearance: Correlated Colour Temperature to be within the range 2900K to 4200K.

Ultraviolet control: Not required.

Infrared control: Not required.

Lighting category L1: Controlled daylight

Lighting category L1 is daylight with illuminance control. Museum visitors in L1 zones should be aware that daylight is the principal source of illumination during normal daylight hours. This awareness aspect is important: visitors should be in no doubt that they are experiencing the exhibits under daylight. The daylight control system must not conceal the source of illumination.

Day or night, exhibition spaces within L1 zones are to appear well-lighted. The lighting will reveal the architecture as well as the exhibits, and will enable visitors to orient themselves readily. Exhibit illuminances are to be controlled to limit annual exposure to 600 kilolux hours per year (Table 9.1) but illuminance fluctuations between 150 and 300 lux are acceptable. The daylight control system is to be capable of totally excluding daylight out of exhibition hours.

Exhibits Exhibits to be placed in an L1 zone need to be composed of materials having either R0 or R1 category (Table 3.1).

It should be noted that illuminance fluctuations are acceptable in an L1 zone but not in an L2 zone. If there is doubt about the ability of an R1 material to withstand such fluctuations, it should be displayed in an L2 zone.

Physical connections Generally, visitors enter an L1 zone from an L0 zone, and then move on to an L2 zone. An L1 zone does not connect directly to an L3 zone.

Visual connections There may be restricted views to the outside from an L1 zone, such as a view to an enclosed courtyard or through to a nearby L0 zone with side glazing, and generally there will be views into L2 zones, as well as to other exhibition spaces within the L1 zone.

Daylight *Glazing:* Skylights are to give access to diffused sky illumination, with total exclusion of direct sunlight. Tinted glazing is not to be used.

Sunlight admission: Nil.

Daylight distribution: In some L1 zones, more or less uniform illuminance will be required over the floor area for exhibiting three-dimensional objects. In others, daylight will be directed onto the walls where paintings and other two-dimensional works are to be hung.

Illuminance control: During normal daylight hours, exhibit illuminance is to be maintained within the range 150 to 300 lux, without manual intervention.

Ultraviolet control: Skylights are to be equipped with a filter medium to effectively eliminate all radiation of wavelength less than 400 nm.

Electric light *Duration of use:* The daytime use of ambient electric lighting is to be minimal, although display lighting may be used to provide selective highlighting. Ambient electric lighting is provided primarily to supplement the daylight on dull days and at night.

Light distributions: An ambient electric lighting system is required both to supplement the daylight illumination on dull days and to provide night-time illumination, and the lighting distribution must be appropriate for these functions. A flexible system of display lighting is also required.

Illuminance control: The ambient lighting control should provide smooth transitions between daylight, daylight supplemented by electric light, and total electric lighting. The ambient lighting system must be able to provide any chosen level of illuminance on the exhibits up to 200 lux. The display lighting system is to be separately controlled so that selective highlighting can supplement either the daylight or the ambient electric lighting.

Colour rendering: General Colour Rendering Index to be not less than 85.

Colour appearance: Correlated Colour Temperature to be within the range 2900K to 4200K. Where different lamp types are used in the same space, colour temperatures must be closely matched.

Ultraviolet control: Effective elimination of radiation of wavelength less than 400 nm is required.

Infrared control: Not required.

Lighting category L2: Restricted exposure

Lighting category L2 is electric lighting for material responsiveness categories up to R2, and comprises both an ambient lighting system and a flexible display lighting system, the two systems being separately controlled. This provides exhibition designers with options ranging from a diffusely illuminated space with selective highlighting, to a darkened interior with dramatic spotlighting.

Where R2 materials are displayed, exhibit illuminance is limited to 50 lux (Table 9.1). This will maintain the annual exposure within 150 kilolux hours per year providing the duration of exposure does not exceed 3000 hours per year.

Where no materials having responsiveness category greater than R1 are displayed, illuminances may be increased up to 200 lux. However, it should be noted that the L1 and L2 zones are not equivalent in the level of protection that they provide. Museum staff should be aware that environmental conditions, including lighting, are less likely to be precisely controlled in L1 zones than in L2 zones. If there is some doubt about a material's ability to withstand some environmental variation, then an L2 zone will be the more appropriate location.

Exhibits Exhibits in an L2 zone may include materials that have up to R2 responsiveness category (Table 3.1).

Physical connections Generally visitors enter an L2 zone from an L0 or L1 zone. They may return to one of those zones or move on to an L3 zone.

Visual connections There will be no direct views to the outside from an L2 zone, but often there will be views into an L0 or an L1 zone, as well as to other exhibition spaces within the L2 zone.

Daylight Nil.

Electric light *Duration of use:* Both the ambient and the display lighting systems will be in use throughout exhibition hours in an L2 zone, and the systems are to be separately controlled.

Light distributions: For exhibition of paintings, the ambient lighting may be directed onto the walls and other hanging surfaces. It is generally preferred that these surfaces be uniformly washed with light rather than that each work be illuminated by a separate spotlight. For three-dimensional artworks, spotlights may be used in combination with ambient lighting to selectively reveal specific characteristics, such as form, roughness, or sheen, or without ambient lighting as the principal source of illumination.

The ambient and the display lighting systems are to be separately controlled. The ambient lighting system's output must enable the ambient illuminance to be maintained at any chosen level up to 200 lux. Control of the display lighting is to enable luminaires to be controlled individually or in groups.

Colour rendering: General Colour Rendering Index to be not less than 85. Where different lamp types are used in the same space, colour temperatures must be closely matched.

Colour appearance: Correlated Colour Temperature to be within the range 2900K to 4200K.

Ultraviolet control: Effective elimination of radiation of wavelength less than 400 nm is required.

Infrared control: Filament spotlights (including halogen) to have dichroic reflectors, or to incorporate filters that restrict infrared radiation onto exhibits.

Lighting category L3: Minimal exposure

Lighting category L3 is electric lighting for all material responsiveness categories including R3, and comprises both an ambient lighting system and a flexible display lighting system, the two systems being separately controlled. Environmental conditions are to be controlled with precision, and light exposure may be reduced to low levels. The approach to an L3 zone should be carefully contrived to provide viewers with progressive adaptation achieved by a gradual transition of reducing brightness, in order to avoid an impression of dullness or gloom upon entering. Use of transition lobbies can be helpful. Both direct and reflected glare are to be eliminated in order to optimize viewing conditions, and any highlighting should be applied with restraint.

Exhibits Exhibits in an L3 zone may include all material responsiveness categories. However, R3 materials require special consideration.

Even where exhibit illuminance values are limited to 50 lux, R3 materials placed on permanent display would exceed the limiting annual exposure of 15 kilolux hours per year (Table 9.1). Strategies need to be devised to prevent this from happening. These strategies may include restricting illuminance to less than 50 lux; having exhibits under covers when not actually being viewed; using motion detectors, time switches or manual switching to restrict exposure duration; or taking exhibits off display at intervals.

Physical connections L3 zones connect only with L2 zones, preferably through a transition lobby.

Visual connections Restricted views to zones having daylight may be possible from an L3 zone, but generally there will only be views through to L2 zones and to other spaces within the L3 zone.

Daylight Nil.

Electric light *Duration of use:* The electric lighting will be in use throughout exhibition hours in an L3 zone.

Light distributions: Separate ambient and display lighting systems should be provided.

Illuminance control: Ambient and display lighting systems are to be separately controlled. The ambient lighting system's output is to be adjustable so that exhibit illuminance can be maintained at any chosen level up to 100 lux. Each display luminaire's output must be individually controllable. Lamp output intensities should be chosen so that when the lamps are at full output and at normal lighting distances, both illuminance and infrared irradiance will comply with specified conservation criteria.

Colour rendering: General Colour Rendering Index to be not less than 85.

Colour appearance: Correlated Colour Temperature to be within the range 2900K to 4200K. Where different lamp types are used in the same space, colour temperatures must be closely matched.

Ultraviolet control: Effective elimination of radiation of wavelength less than 400 nm is required.

Infrared control: Filament spotlights (including halogen) to have dichroic reflectors, or must incorporate filters to restrict infrared radiation on exhibits.

Other lighting systems

As explained in the Introduction, all exhibition spaces are to have provision for ambient, display, cleaners', security, and emergency lighting. This may require five separately controlled lighting systems, although opportunities for shared functions should be considered.

The design of ceilings to incorporate the lighting systems will require close collaboration with the architects, the museum staff, and the providers of other services, particularly the air conditioning. The need to achieve appropriate illumination distributions with glare avoidance will be a major determinant of the ceiling profiles in the daylit galleries.

It is intended that the electric lighting systems will, as far as is practical, be unobtrusive. Some compromises between flexibility, accessibility, and concealment of the display lighting systems are inevitable, but ceilings cluttered with luminaires should be avoided.

The performance requirements for the ambient and display lighting have been detailed in the foregoing sections, and the principal factors are summarized briefly in Table 9.2. Also, the critical aspect of connections between different zones of the exhibition spaces is illustrated diagrammatically in Figure 9.1. Requirements for the other systems are given in the following subsections.

Cleaners' lighting

The system is to comprise an unobtrusive installation of recessed luminaires arranged so that the light output will be directed onto the floor, with minimal direct illumination of exhibits. The illuminance on the floor is to be not less than 200 lux. Manual switching controls are to be provided for use by the cleaners, and there is to be a clear policy that this lighting is to be used only when cleaning is in progress.

Security lighting

Requirements will depend upon the security procedures, including whether or not the museum is to be patrolled at night, and the operational requirements of any security cameras. Modern colour monitor cameras can operate satisfactorily in ambient illuminance levels less than 1 lux, and the most important aspect of lighting is to provide even, well-diffused illumination that avoids strong shadows and reflections of light sources in shiny surfaces. Generally, indirect lighting is favoured, and luminaire locations should be determined with regard for camera locations to minimize the probability of reflections in troublesome surfaces, such as dark-coloured polished floors. Some security procedures rely on constant monitoring, and others rely on the museum being in total darkness with the cameras set to detect any light, so that security staff can be alerted to the presence of an intruder. In such cases, the lighting is controlled from the security room.

Emergency lighting

Emergency lighting and egress signs are to comply with current standards and recommendations. It is generally recommended that the illuminance on the floor should be not less than 1 lux.

Setting up lighting for a new exhibition

Planning for progressive adaptation

Museum staff who have responsibility for lighting are likely to be confronted by conflicts with exhibitions designers and others who want to have materials displayed in locations where it may seem impossible both to achieve effective visual display and to restrict light exposure to levels demanded by the maximum responsiveness category of the materials. At these times a clearly stated museum lighting policy is valuable, but still solutions may have to be negotiated for some difficult situations.

The higher the R category, the more likely are the problems. The previous chapter has described the process of progressive adaptation, and ideally all visitors will pass through the sequence of lighting categories shown in Figure 9.1 on their way to locations where R3 and R4 materials are displayed. In reality, many factors can make this difficult to achieve. In a multi-storey museum, the only L0 and L1 lighting conditions are likely to be on the top-lit upper floor, and it is almost as likely that the only way to enter the museum will be through the ground floor level galleries, which offer the only opportunities to provide L3 lighting conditions. Art exhibitions are often organized chronologically, so that the oldest display objects, which often are the most responsive, are the first exhibits to be encountered. Progressive adaptation can be hard to provide.

The objective is to lead people into a low ambient illumination location without them sensing gloom, and ways of achieving progressive adaptation to low ambient light levels have been discussed in Chapter 8, p. 231. The measures include avoiding a direct view into a less bright location, and for this a route that follows a zig-zag path with progressively reducing light levels can be very effective, particularly if it is arranged so that something of interest and relevance is presented for view at the end of each leg of the route. Visitors to an exhibition will usually stop to read introductory text, and if this can be broken down into sections that are short enough to avoid obstructions being formed along the route, visitors will have time to adapt to the reducing light levels. Care has to be taken to avoid conditions that might threaten safety, and in some parts of the world there are specified minimum light levels that must be provided at all times. Usually these are specified in terms of illuminance on the floor, which can be provided by recessed miniature luminaires mounted at low level. It may be noted that it is usually illuminance, rather than exitance, that is specified, so that dark-coloured floor and wall materials can satisfy such requirements while adapting viewers to low ambient conditions. Even so, it would be prudent to ensure that changes of direction are clearly indicated by light-coloured skirting and changes of level by light-coloured stair nosings.

Viewers must feel relaxed and comfortable if they are to give their attention to the displays, and low ambient light levels need special attention. The use of light-coloured handrails is advisable, particularly where low-level luminaires are used. Otherwise, my own recommendation is that the mean room surface exitance values should be not less than 3 lux. This may not seem to be much, but remember this is illuminance measured at the eye excluding direct light, so that it takes account only of light reflected from surrounding surfaces. When lighting is measured in this way, it is surprising how few lux we need to see our surroundings perfectly well. Guidance on this metric is given in Chapter 2.

Lighting the displays

It is very important to have confidence in the R categories for all the materials to be displayed. This means that all materials, including colourants and varnishes, have been correctly identified, and that their responsiveness has been correctly classified, and only a professional conservator has the skill to do this reliably. The conservator's decisions may cause difficulties for the lighting designer. For example, it may become necessary to set up a controlled daylight gallery (L2 category) as a restricted exposure (L3) location, to enable all the responsive materials to be appropriately displayed. The earlier in the process that these issues can be discussed with the exhibitions designer, the better.

Enough has been said in the foregoing pages to make it clear that there is a lot more to lighting than providing prescribed illuminance values. Ambient illumination, and whether or not spaces are daylit, strongly influence display lighting options. The extent to which appreciation of the displayed objects depends on recognition of form or texture, or on discrimination of detail or colour, or of transparency or lustre, demand careful consideration. Do the objects have glossy surface characteristics, and if so, is this to be revealed, as for polished wood or glazed porcelain, or not, as for a glazed picture or a glossy photograph? All of these factors are the concerns of the lighting designer, and no matter how experienced that person may be, setting up, aiming and adjusting the lighting is a time-consuming process that must not be rushed. It is necessary that the important visual attributes of the objects are effectively revealed.

The illuminance levels for responsive materials require careful consideration. A lighting designer who starts from the standpoint that the aim is to reveal effectively the visual attributes of the displayed objects with minimum incident light, quickly discovers that some objects need more light than others. Furthermore, this need can be affected by changing the surroundings. Background lightness and colour are influential in ways that depend on the material being displayed. Sometimes a strong contrast is effective, as when clear glassware is displayed on a dark background (see Figure 2.12(e)), and in other situations it is beneficial to minimize contrast. Watercolour paintings tend to benefit from being displayed on a background that matches them closely for overall lightness and colour tone. Generally, paintings appear darkened when hung on a light-coloured surface, and a similar darkening occurs when there is glare, direct or reflected, in the field of view. By overcoming such darkening effects, there may be opportunity to reduce incident light, and this approach contributes both to visibility and to conservation.

Illuminance limits and exposure limits

The limiting illuminance values in Table 9.1 are not targets, but guides for practice. For the R1 and R2 categories, the limiting exposure values are based on the notion that 3000 hours of exposure per year is typical for objects on permanent display. It follows that materials that are classified R3 must not be placed on permanent display, assuming that nobody would attempt to display an object at 5 lux. This means that museums have to institute procedures for restricting the duration of exposure for highly responsive materials, which may involve permitting some objects to be displayed only in short-duration exhibitions, or rotating objects between display and storage, or having some parts of the museum open only for restricted hours.

Consider a R2 object for which, no matter how carefully we arrange the lighting and the surroundings, the least illuminance that reveals its essential visual attributes is 120 lux. It is not acceptable to put this responsive material on display and to blame its poor appearance on the 50 lux limiting illuminance value, for this is the worst of all worlds. The object is being damaged by exposure, and nobody is getting any satisfaction from seeing it. The approach to take is to acknowledge that whenever a responsive material is put on display, some part of its useful life will be used up. It is the collective responsibility of those who put it on display to ensure both that the used-up part of its life will be no larger than necessary, and that it will be used to good effect. In this case, we must illuminate the object to 120 lux, but it has to be done with the agreement of all concerned that the hours of exposure will be logged, and when it comes off display, it will go into storage for sufficient time to restore the limiting annual exposure. For example, if the object is displayed for 2000 hours at 120 lux, the cumulative exposure is 240 000 lx h (lux hours). The limiting annual exposure is 150 000 lx h/y, so this is the exposure that may accumulate over 240 000/150 000 = 1.6 years, or 19.2 months. If the actual period of display is to be 8 months, when the object comes off display it will have to go into storage for at least 11.2 months.

Alternatively, what happens when we encounter an R2 object that appears well presented at 35 lux? The answer is that for this object, which probably is light in colour and reflects a high proportion of incident light, we have a conservation bonus. The object should be displayed at 35 lux, and it should be passed on to succeeding generations in better condition than it would have been if we had unthinkingly applied the 50 lux limiting illuminance.

Checking for UV and IR

It is necessary to check for ultraviolet radiation, and as has been explained in Chapter 3, the aim is total elimination. Start by checking that all light has entered the space either through glass or clear plastic, as this will ensure elimination of wavelengths shorter than 315 nm. Be particularly careful to check tungsten halogen lamps, ensuring that if they do not have integral glass covers, hard glass covers are installed that are capable of retaining parts from a shattered lamp. A UV meter that covers the range 315 to 400 nm is a useful tool, not for measuring the UV, but for detecting its presence. Every source of light, including daylight, should be equipped with a UV filter, but the performance of these filters can deteriorate over time. If the meter shows a response, it can be used to trace the source. Sometimes filters are inadvertently omitted when lamps are changed.

It is advisable also to check for radiant heating effect, particularly where incandescent filament spotlights are in use. The culprit is infrared radiation, but hand-held IR meters are not available. The simple procedure to check the heating effect at the object is to feel the effect on the back of your hand. If it seems to be significant, and particularly if the displayed objects are likely to be susceptible, such as those discussed in Chapter 3, remedial action is necessary. If practical, switch to lamps with dichroic reflectors, otherwise add IR heat filters.

It remains to ensure that whoever will maintain the installation has all the information they need to maintain the lighting effect that has been painstakingly achieved, and to ensure that the exhibits will not be exposed unnecessarily.

Maintaining lighting during the life of an exhibition

Daily checks are necessary to ensure replacement of failed lamps, but from time to time more careful checks are required to ensure that the initial conditions are being maintained.

It is not unusual for the the person who has responsibility for maintaining exhibition lighting to have had little or no involvement in setting up the installation. Sometimes designers return to the scene of their creative work after an interval and are disappointed to find that the lighting is out of adjustment and is not giving the display appearance that they had initially achieved. They blame the maintenance staff, but they should consider whether they had ensured that the staff fully understood the purpose of the lighting and how it had been balanced to achieve this. Also, had the designer provided written instructions for routine maintenance? Designers who fail on these counts have themselves to blame for future shortcomings.

Maintenance staff should know the correct distribution of illuminances, and should check this periodically, particularly where discharge lamps, such as metal halide, or LEDs are used. Unlike tungsten halogen lamps, which maintain their light output until end of life failure, these light sources can continue to operate for long periods with progressively reducing light output. The UV meter should also be used to check that filters have not deteriorated or been omitted when lamps have been changed. Any signs of localized heating should be investigated. Perhaps an IR filter has been omitted, or a dichroic reflector lamp has been replaced with an aluminium reflector lamp.

Finally the operation of the control system should be checked. As controls become highly automated, so it becomes more important to have good information on how they are operating. Maintenance staff should be able to check that the display lighting has been operating only during viewing hours, that the cleaners' lighting has not been in use more than necessary, and that use of the security lighting has been in accordance with policy. A log of maintenance inspections should be maintained.

References

Ashley-Smith, J. (1999) *Risk Assessment for Object Conservation.* Butterworth-Heinemann

Boud, J. K. (1971) Lighting for effect. *Light & Lighting*, **64**, 230

Cuttle, C. (2003) *Lighting by Design*. Architectural Press

Knoblauch, K. et al. (1987) Age and illuminance effects in the Farnsworth-Munsell 100-hue test. *Applied Optics*, **26**(8), 1441–48

Loe, D.L., Rowlands, E., and Watson, N.F. (1982) Preferred lighting conditions for the display of oil and watercolour paintings. *Lighting Res. Technol.*, **14**(4), 173–192

Lynes, J.A., and Cuttle, C. (1988) Bracelet for total solar shading. *Lighting Res. Technol.*, **20**(3), 105–113

Phillips, D. (1971). In discussion of Lynes, J.A. *Lighting Res. Technol.*, **3**(1), 24, p.39

Bibliography

Museum lighting guides

CIE 157:2004 *Control of Damage to Museum Objects by Optical Radiation.* International Commission on Illumination, Vienna

LG8: 1994 *Lighting for Museums and Art Galleries.* Chartered Institution of Building Services Engineers, London

RP-30-96 *Museum and Art Gallery Lighting: A Recommended Practice.* Illuminating Engineering Society of North America, New York

Lighting practice and lighting design

Boyce, P. (2003) *Human Factors in Lighting,* 2nd edition. Taylor and Francis

Coaton, J.R., and Marsden, A.M. (eds) (1997) *Lamps and Lighting,* 4th edition. Arnold

Cuttle, C. (2003) *Lighting by Design.* Architectural Press

Major, M., Speirs, J., and Tischhauser, A. (2005) *Made of Light: The Art of Light and Architecture.* Birkhâuser

Rea, M. (ed) (2000) *Lighting Handbook,* 9th edition. Illuminating Engineering Society of North America, New York

Simons R.H. and Bean. A.R. (2001) *Lighting Engineering: Applied Calculations.* Architectural Press

Daylighting practice

Ander, G.D. (1995) *Daylighting Performance and Design.* Van Nostrand Reinhold

Button D.A., and Pye, B. (eds) (1993) *Glass in Building: A guide to modern architectural glass performance.* Butterworth Architecture

International Energy Agency (2000) *Daylight in Buildings: A source book on daylighting systems and components.* A report of IEA SHC Task 21/ECBCS Annex 29, http://www.iea.shc.org

Moore, F. (1991) *Concepts and Practice of Architectural Daylighting.* Van Nostrand Reinhold

Conservation

Ashley-Smith, J. (1999) *Risk Assessment for Object Conservation.* Butterworth-Heinemann

Horie, C.V. (2005) *Materials for Conservation.* Butterworth-Heinemann

Keene, S. (2002) *Managing Conservation in Museums, 2nd edition.* Butterworth-Heinemann

Thomson, G. (2003) *The Museum Environment,* 2nd edition. Butterworth-Heinemann

Viñas, S.M. (2005) *Contemporary Theory of Conservation.* Elsevier

Index